Jackie,

Edge of Sanity

You are a special lady.
May God bless you.

Marlene R. Lovejoy

Edge of Sanity

Journal of Depression, Bipolar Disorder, and Beyond

Marlene Russell Lovejoy

VANTAGE PRESS
New York

The opinions expressed herein are solely those of the author. Readers should seek the advice of their personal physician, therapist, or caregiver before changing or entering into any form of psychiatric assistance.

Excerpts from *The Anxiety & Phobia Workbook, 4th Edition,* by Edmund Bourne, is reprinted with permission by New Harbinger Publications, Inc. (www.newharbinger.com).

Cover design by Polly McQuillen

FIRST EDITION

All rights reserved, including the right of reproduction in whole or in part in any form.

Published by Vantage Press, Inc.
419 Park Ave. South, New York, NY 10016

Manufactured in the United States of America
ISBN: 978-0-533-15674-0

Library of Congress Catalog Card No.: 2006909761

0 9 8 7 6 5 4 3 2

To my family,
my children, Ashley and Tyler,
and my wonderful husband, Ben

Out of suffering have emerged the strongest souls.

—E.H. Chapin

Contents

Acknowledgments		xi
Introduction		xiii
Author's Note		xv

One	Overload	1
Two	Darkness Falls	7
Three	Strange Things	18
Four	Outpouring	21
Five	Help	26
Six	Earlier Manifestations	30
Seven	The Switch	32
Eight	The Shrink	37
Nine	More Panic Attacks	44
Ten	Second Shrink Visit	52
Eleven	The Mental Ward	63
Twelve	The Release	100
Thirteen	Explanations and Clarifications	106

Endnotes	129
Bibliography	133

Acknowledgments

Many thanks to everyone who helped me along the way: my doctor, the nurses, and every staff member at the hospital whose healing words and care lifted me from a world of darkness and fear.

A world of gratitude goes to my daughter and son who have always been my inspiration; to my steadfast parents and brother; to my dear sisters, who not only shared their insights throughout the writing process, but also survived the doctor's visits; and to my husband, Ben, who is the love of my life.

Introduction

For years I have wanted to write a book about living with depression, and bipolar disorder. After considerable contemplation of its contents, I dared to include my stay in a mental ward. My difficulties in writing have included staying on task, writing clearly, and not losing interest. Fortunately, I jotted down notes on scraps of paper, kept daily journals, and made tapes throughout my ordeal since my memory was sketchy.

The account is based on my phenomonology, i.e., "the world" as I perceived it at that time. My "reality,"or what *I* was experiencing, may have seemed different to others with whom I was interacting. If the account seems distorted and jumbled, then that was my perception at the time.

Hopefully, my experiences will be therapeutic and beneficial for those who can relate or identify with these issues. Millions of Americans today are suffering with similar disorders of depression, or some type of mood affective disorder. Living in the 21st century, we are fortunate to have as much medical help and acceptance as we do. Even in our sophisticated society, most people still speak in whispers about mental health issues.

In times past, many people were locked away in insane asylums with mental disorders such as ours. People were ashamed of family members with mental problems. Unfortunately, these persons identified as "crazy," "mad," or "insane" were treated inhumanely—given shock treatments without pain relief, tied to their beds, kept overly sedated, or naked. They lived out their lives in confinement within a lunatic asylum or mental hospital.

The main purpose of this account is to speak to people, using everyday language, about these mental health disorders. Hopefully, I can provide a clearer understanding of these topics as well as dispel many misconceptions.

I have not overcome my disorder, but manage the symptoms through my "wellness patterns" . . . daily medication, healthy diet, regular exercise, prayer, and psychiatric therapy sessions. The continual balancing act of my mind and body are tedious, and a daily struggle. Just ask my family and friends.

Author's Note

How did I end up here? A mental institution conjures up the worst mental images one can possibly imagine . . . strait jackets, padded cells, zombie-like patients wandering the halls, electric shock treatments with sterile, gray walls and rooms filled with endless screaming. Most of the movies we have seen have the patients taking over the hospital or asylum, and murdering the staff with butcher knives. Needless to say, entering a mental hospital was one of the scariest moments of my life.

My mind was racing with thoughts; then, I realized someone was speaking. . . .

"Are you suicidal at this moment?" the clerk inquired.

"Yes, yes, I am."

The room seemed too quiet as I looked around seeing the doors leading to a world completely unknown to me. My heart was in my throat, but my brain was in a logical mode, at least, for a moment. I knew I had to enter this place to get help, although my hands were soaked in sweat, thinking about the unknown lying ahead.

"Why are you so afraid?" she asked.

"Well, O.K., tell me one movie or book about mental hospitals that you have ever seen that doesn't scare you to death."

She just stared at me. "This place is *not* like that."

"How am I supposed to know that?"

"They will take good care of you."

She seemed too calm and self-assured; maybe, she was bored with her job.

"How do I know what ya'll are going to do to me?"

"You will be fine . . . now, if you will sign these forms, we can get you checked in."

Oh, great, I thought, *I have finally lost it [sic, my mind]. How in the world did I end up here?*

Edge of Sanity

One

Overload

By the fall of 1997, at the age of forty-seven, many years of stressful events had begun to take their toll on me . . . episodes of depression, a rocky marriage, a miscarriage, a son with special health issues, divorce, remarriage, on and on. Intertwined with that were my own health problems which included a hysterectomy, fibromyalgia, and neurofibromatosis. Also, I had been going to doctors everywhere for pain in my neck and back from two car accidents. Cortizone injections with lidocaine had provided temporary relief. Finally, I tried acupuncture which had been a tremendous solution to alleviate my pain; however, it was not covered by insurance. During all those traumatic times I had seen counselors and therapists, who kept me afloat. In addition, my quest to be a super Mom to a blended family of four children, dealing with the normal midlife issues, and working fulltime had become a definite overload.

My daughter, Ashley, was in college. She and I were very close, and I missed our times together—sitting on the bed for hours still in our pajamas, talking and drinking coffee; or making pecan pralines for Christmas gifts, which we mostly ate; or decorating for Christmas and singing carols, which she wholeheartedly enjoyed. True togetherness. As much as I had always wanted her to grow up and be independent, I was not ready for her to actually leave.

At work I had my share of troubles. I felt overwhelmed with

my workload, as more and more duties were added. My supervisor would call me in for a little *chat,* which usually meant more work.

"Marlene, how are things going?"

"Good, except for feeling swamped with work. Trying to cover my area, assist in another area, plus some weekend and night work is consuming me. I just have too much. Plus, ya'll let my student assistant go because of lack of funding."

"Well, you are doing a good job. So, now, we have another little project for you."

Apparently, he had not heard a word I said. My stomach started to cramp. The harder you work, the more you get done, and the more they give you to do. Why do I work so hard?

"Do I get paid more?"

(Soft chuckle.) "No, this project is considered 'other duties as assigned.' "

At first, I talked about it calmly in a matter-of-fact way. With most people, I could communicate and reach an agreement. With him, my words did not make any difference . . . like talking to a brick wall. At times, he and I had difficulties reaching any level of compromise or understanding.

Out of the blue, a wave of anger began to rise up from my stomach; almost, instantaneously, a very strange sensation swirled inside my brain causing me to feel extremely agitated. A word he had spoken or his general attitude set me off. Something had suddenly ticked me off with no warning. I did not feel like myself. Anger flowed upward through my chest, arms and face. I felt lightheaded. I took a very deep breath, as my upper body puffed up and tightened, like an animal switching to "fight mode." My heart began to pound so loudly, that I was sure my supervisor could hear it.

What was happening to me? I felt that it was not me, but someone else . . . almost the way you feel in a dream. You are not totally there; somebody else has taken control. My face was hot . . . I looked down . . . my fists were clinched. I was consumed with anger . . . agitation . . . then, rage. Ready to explode. I wanted to yell at him.

My thoughts were racing like wildfire through my head, *Since I am overwhelmed with my workload, he will respond by giving me more to do. Does he care? But, it really did not matter. I did not have a choice in the matter. Just stop arguing and do what he says.*

Then, I heard the aggravated tone of *my* voice. It did not seem like the usual, cordial me. I knew what I was saying but could not believe I was saying it. Normally, I was considered a good person, and a well-mannered Southern lady.

"You continue to give me more and more." The words poured out in a torrent. "Do you expect me to do it quietly without saying anything?"

"Marlene, you need to realize . . ."

I cut him off and kept going. "Also, you always treat us (the staff) like we are below you since we do not have such and such degree. You are always talking down to us. Well, I have had it." I ranted and raved on and on.

Afterwards, as I trudged back to my office, I felt mentally and physically spent . . . very down and depressed. Uncontrollable tears came pouring down my face. I could not stop crying. I felt like a fool, ashamed of my behavior. My mind was in a dark place, and I could not extricate the horrible "down" feeling.

Simultaneously, thoughts were flying through my brain . . . all jumbled and out-of-control. I continued to replay the entire conversation in my mind over and over. Very negative self-talk was in high gear . . . *Why am I acting like this? Why did I lash out?* I continued to beat myself up mentally and fussed at myself about acting so crazy and unprofessional. I just kept punching away internally, and becoming more miserable; but, I could not stop.

But, of course, I always did the work or project I was assigned. On my yearly evaluation, my supervisor gave me ratings of "excellent" or "exceptional," in most areas. In the "comments section" of the evaluation, he wrote "she is an outstanding employee, except for these occasional periods of 'incongruent behavior.' " Another time he wrote that she has "a quirk" in her personality.

These incongruent episodes began to occur more often, and I never knew when or where one would happen. After it was over, I felt embarrassed. I hated these agitated outbursts, but I was clueless about their cause or onset. However, I was not even aware of these episodes being a real problem for a long time . . . i.e., as far as sitting down to analyze or solve them.

Then, on April 1, a sad thing occurred at work. A co-worker had a massive heart attack in the middle of a grievance committee meeting. No one knew if it was brought on by the stress of the situation, but a week later, she died. She was one of the most respected librarians in the state. Her office was ten feet from mine. We were all deeply saddened by her passing.

(From notes.) By June, signs of depression (although I was not aware) had started sneaking in . . . overly emotional more and more often; feelings of exhaustion; restless sleep, and irritability. Started feeling "the darkness within" for longer periods of time; sometimes, two or more weeks; extremely agitated at the least little thing. Later on, I labeled this state of mind, as 'sliding down the slippery slope.'

Also, at work I remembered sitting at my computer one day; I began to experience a unique sensation within my head. A strange sort of lightheadedness. But not like any feeling I had before . . . very hard to describe . . . maybe, a little dizzy. It was almost as if my eyes and brain were set back an inch away from my skull, and I became extremely preoccupied with my thoughts. Did not feel like myself, but almost as if I was watching myself. Very conscious of this new, strange sensation. I became so uneasy about these new developments swirling within my brain that I left work. I took sick leave for the afternoon and headed home.

In addition, my thirteen-year-old son moved in with his dad, who lived two hours away. Everyone assured me that a teenage boy's natural inclination was to connect with his dad. Especially alluring for him was the fact that his dad was a coach.

Because of his health issues, Ty and I had spent many hours together on doctors' visits, and long stays at Shriner's hospital. Consequently, I felt we had a close bond. Due to a rare bone disorder, Ty's foot was amputated a month before his sixth birthday. Six months later, his prosthesis had liberated him, and he had taken off. He actually coped extremely well.

Fortunately, my parents went on all the trips with us even buying a station wagon to accommodate his surgeries, equipment and toys. Also, we had the prayers and support of my family, friends and hundreds of church members praying, calling, sending cards and gifts.

However, I thought I would lose my mind. I began to undergo intensive psychotherapy to survive the trauma of his horrendous surgeries and amputation.

His older sister, Ashley, nurtured him and loved him dearly. When he was little, she slung him on her hip and took him all over the neighborhood playing with all the kids. She was an integral part in helping him face life in a positive way, continually encouraging and supporting him in everything he did.

Now, seven years had passed and nothing had slowed him down. He played every sport possible, and was an inspiration to everyone he knew. But, now, he was moving away. His leaving filled my heart with hurt and sadness, but I kept all the pain inside. Determined not to sway his feelings, I did not mention to him how I felt. He had to make his own decisions now.

Besides, I was used to hiding my feelings; I had done it my entire life. It was a mask that I wore, most of the time . . . the "everything is fine" mask. I was an expert at holding all my emotions and feelings within.

September 12–14, 1997

By age three, Ty's dad was teaching him to swing a golf club. Golf might be easier for him than other sports. Even though he always had a cast or brace on, he kept playing. By age ten Ty had joined a group of amputee golfers. Of course, he was the youngest one by far, but he enjoyed the yearly tournaments and camaraderie with the other golfers he met. Every fall the amputee golf tournament was held in different states. This year Ash and I took Ty to play in Pell City, Alabama. Apparently, ragweed was in full bloom as we walked around the course all weekend. So, by Sunday afternoon, my allergies had kicked into high gear. It was a normal occurrence for me to start sneezing, and become congested in mid-September, almost like clockwork every year.

Two

Darkness Falls

Monday, September 15

By Monday, I had developed a terrible sinus infection and congestion. I felt miserable; could not breathe, could not sleep. I did not
go to work, but I called my general MD. When I went in for the appointment that day, he prescribed an antibiotic and decongestant.

"Dr. Dillon, can you change my antidepressant medicine,
too? I have been feeling very depressed again."

"Well, it is not a good idea to change your other medicines
while you are sick. Your body is handling enough right now."

"I know . . . I was afraid you would say that."

"Besides, Marlene, you realize that there is no magic pill.
Most depressions come in cycles, and there are so many outside
influences which affect it."

"I know, I know . . . I am not looking for a magical solution. I
just need to be able to feel well enough to function."

After several more convincing statements, he relented,
"Well, O.K. maybe you can try Serzone. Just be aware that it is a
different type of antidepressant."

"Thank you, I know I will start feeling better."

"Stop taking your Effexor and Elavil (I was taking low dosages of each) immediately. Here are some sample packets for you
to begin the Serzone so you can see how you do. Start with 100
mg. in the morning and at night. And, for sleep, take one tablet (10

mg.) of Ambien at night." (Keep in mind, he was a general practitioner.)

I was feeling horrible. My nerves seem raw and exposed . . . hard to explain; don't know how much longer I can hold on. . . . Deep emptiness.

Unless you have suffered with depression, you cannot begin to imagine how it is. Like an iron clad vise, this thing was squeezing me; its grip would not let me escape. I wanted to leave the scary unknown world of darkness that I was trapped in. Darkness had become an overwhelming, stifling blackness that was consuming me.

Wednesday, September 17, 1997

Two days passed, and I got worse. My journal notes, again:

. . . I cannot cope any longer . . . I'm so overwhelmed by anything and everything. Miserably low. I feel like the darkness has now taken over my insides. Verge of suicide. Deep depression . . . Did not want to cope (with) anything any longer, wanted to be done with life, didn't care, needed help deseparately (sic) (I am losing the ability to even spell words correctly). . . . Confused . . .

Why do I keep fighting this depression? Who knows? Maybe, my destiny is to end it all.

Dear God, please help me!!

Thursday, September 18

Had cancelled plans to eat out with friends or attend party on Saturday night. No possible way I could mingle with people . . . could no longer pretend things were O.K.

My family and friends continued to call constantly. They were all very worried about me. Repeatedly, I remember telling them I was suffering from a "nervous breakdown" which was a term everyone at that time used to cover any mental problem. Of course, exactly what constituted a "nervous breakdown" was unclear to me. I actually looked this condition up in my encyclopedia. (This was before the onslaught of the Internet.) Found a very brief and vague definition. . . .

"nervous breakdown: a mental or emotional disorder, especially of a sufficient nature to require hospitalization."

(Part of a letter, I wrote during this period of time.)

"Very sick and depressed. I seem to be worrying excessively . . . Head congestion—all stopped [up]. Could not stop crying for 2–3 hours. Was ready to hold a gun to my head. Cried uncontrollably. Intense feelings of nothingness . . . emptiness. Felt alone, and not worthy of living. Felt that some people would not care if I was dead. Not sure that they would even cry. Didn't feel like anyone loved me . . . maybe, Ash, Ty, or my family. A few friends would miss me, but they would get over it, after a while. Life would go on. My job would go on easily without me.

"I have just given so much of myself my whole life, and life has been too overwhelming for me. I have been hurt too much. (I cried as I was writing).

"I grew up thinking I was not good enough. I had little confidence in myself . . . low self-esteem. I was a very sensitive child, and my feelings were easily hurt. And, no matter how hard I tried, I felt I could not measure up to what was expected."

This letter went on and on for pages about the problems within my first marriage:

"Wanted more than anything to be loved, but felt unworthy. Maybe, I thought I had to work hard to earn love. Felt I was always to be blamed for not getting the love I needed. I don't know exactly why. Felt very alone in my first marriage.

"Then, my son being born with some difficult health issues overwhelmed me, and threw me in to almost two years of depression. Cried for days, could not sleep, lost weight because I could not eat; continued to work every day, got up every night with Ty. on and on, endless days and nights.

"When my first marriage ended, again felt like a failure. I

9

again had given so much to the marriage. Felt I had received very little love and attention in return.

"Now, I am beginning to feel the same again. I am alone. I will never be worthy of anyone's love. Dying will be the end of my pain and suffering. I am afraid it will hurt others. That is the only reason I have not ended it all yet."

[End of letter.]

The letter was like opening Pandora's box with all of the bad events rushing out, and the words just poured out all over the pages, like a torrent. Everything I wrote seemed to point back to me and my feeling like a failure. Eleven pages of sadness, disappointment and trauma.

During these difficult days, I prayed, and read the Bible as I had always done . . . begging God for answers to my situation. Continually asking God, *What is happening to me?*"

Friday, September 19

My son Ty came home Friday for a weekend visit. Also, my stepson Tyler came from his mother's house. I really don't remember *anything* about that weekend. According to my notes, my husband took them to play golf Saturday.

Saturday, Sept. 20

Had already cancelled plans to attend Sunday school party tonight.Totally out of the question to even think about attending.

Monday, September 22

According to my calendar, I went back to work at the library. (Would not have remembered it at all, if it had not been on my daily calendar.)

Journal notes:

Tried to work . . . exhausted . . . could not concentrate . . . Ringing of phone; became highly agitated. Called doctor to get in to see him and get medicine refilled (Antibiotic and Ambien, for infection and sleep) . . . Constantly worried about running out of medicine.

Numerous phone calls . . . every time phone rings, sets my nerves on edge . . . want to scream.

Tuesday, Sept. 23

Went to work, but overwhelmed . . . Irritated . . . Difficulty concentrating on anything.

Was mad at the doctor for giving me such a small amount of Ambien. Surely, he knew I would exhaust the supply in no time. (Ambien helps with sleeping problems.) Must get an appointment to return. Cannot get my mind off of running out of my medicine.

That evening a thought hit me like a ton of bricks. Of course, it was now as clear as a bell—I realized why the doctor gave me only five tablets of Ambien for sleep. He thought I might decide to overdose. He was aware that I was suicidal, after all. I had not given him sufficient credit.

Wednesday, September 24

Worked my scheduled time. Barely managed to control my emotions all day; a major effort to stifle the tears. I was still sick with the congestion. I was sinking mentally instead of improving.

I went in to see my doctor that afternoon. Dr. Dillon walked in, and we exchanged hellos.

"Doctor, I am still sick, and my medicine is almost gone; and, I cannot handle a relapse. Also, you were right about not changing my antidepressant medicine during a time I was sick. You tried to warn me and talk me out of it. But, I thought I could not feel any worse. You also explained that Serzone would be very different from Elavil and Effexor. I have taken the Serzone since Monday before last. Knowing that it might take several weeks, I have tried to be patient. I do still believe it will help me. At different intervals, I have felt better."

"Yes. Marlene, the thing is . . . we know so little about depression . . . probably only the tip of the iceberg. Doctors *do* know much more than before, but it is difficult to treat for many reasons. We do realize depression is cyclical, and that individual symptoms and problems vary widely. It is hard to find the correct medicine and proper dosage, plus the process is trial and error . . . it takes time."

"Well, I don't know what is happening to me, but I cannot stop crying. I just want to sleep. I am miserable and exhausted. I don't care about anything. When I stopped the Elavil and Effexor 'cold turkey,' my body began to go through the deepest depression I've experienced in a long time. Even though I expected it to be bad; it was horrible. Monday night and Wednesday night I was on the verge of suicide. Uncontrollable crying, night sweats, chills, and fever. Tossing and turning all night. . . . Inability to sleep since my sinuses were stopped up. It was overwhelming."

"Is there a history of depression in your family?"

"No, I am not aware of any. Oh, but I do remember that my grandmother had a nervous breakdown after my grandfather died. I don't know if depression was a part of that, though."

"Have you discussed your situation with anyone?"

"No, not much. I've told my family I'm believe I having a nervous breakdown. But, I guess I am a 'silent sufferer.' (I thought to myself . . . *That is how our generation was raised. Even if we are suffering, we grin and bear it. We are tough, and do not express how we really feel. If anyone asks, the automatic answer is fine . . . no matter what.*)

"But, Marlene, suffering in silence is extremely unhealthy for you. You need to verbalize your feelings . . . let out your frustrations and inability to cope, at times."

"You are right, but I believe most people with depression suffer in silence. We think we should handle our own problems without asking for help. If we seek help, people think we are weak," I said. "Even when I am down, I try to act like I am O.K. . . . you know, happy."

He continued, "Well, 'silent suffering' is great socially . . . everyone likes to be around happy, positive people. However, *acting happy* is not good for you; those pent-up emotions and feelings need to be expressed."

"Doctor, I have always had difficulty expressing anything. I really don't know how to express anger or frustration so I guess I keep it in. Right now, I wish I could control what is going on in my brain; I have read that it could be an imbalance of hormones, or chemicals; but, whatever it is that is going on, I do know I am *not* crazy."

"I believe you are going to be all right. I am prescribing another round of antibiotics, and more Ambien for sleep. Stay on the Serzone a little longer to see if it helps. Call me next week, and let me know how you are doing."

"Thank you. I am lucky to have a caring doctor like you."

He realized I was suffering. But, he did not realize my fragile and dangerous state of mind. I guess he had always known me as a fun-loving, Christian person and could not imagine my being in crisis.

(From a tape recording of myself during the weeks at home.)

"I am going to record my thoughts on tape when I am 'down' so I can express how bad it is. Others can hear the tone of my voice and sense how overwhelming depression can be. Maybe, I can help others later on. I know I can empathize with people; so many people are probably suffering, just like me. (My voice begins in a normal tone but quickly I began to cry.) I cannot say everything I want to say on this tape because of my children. . . . I would not do anything to hurt them. When I talked with my doctor a while back, he thought I should stay on the same medicine a while longer. So, I did. But I did not get any better. I really thought I could not feel any worse; well, I was wrong, *very* wrong. I have gone into a deep depression (I started to cry uncontrollably) . . . knowing that it was part of withdrawing from one medicine and beginning a new one.

13

And last week, I was on the verge of suicide. For days now, I cannot stop crying. . . . I don't know what to do. Sorry, I have to stop taping now." . . . (sobbing uncontrollably).

(When I listened to this tape seven years later, I realized that I said the wrong date: instead of September 24, I said January 24. I had begun to get times, dates and words more confused, but did not always realize it.)

Thurs, Sept. 25

Ten days had passed since my first doctor's visit. I could not get out of bed, or stop crying. Absolutely no energy or interest in anything. . . . I was touchy, irritable, and extremely agitated . . . cancelled more plans . . . could not go to any public place and attempt to act 'normal.'

Read an interesting article in the local newspaper[1] where work had begun on the old cemetery at the mental hospital in Milledgeville (town where we live). Was overgrown with weeds, and hundreds of markers were displaced leaving the graves of patients unmarked.

Phoned a friend about the article.

"Hey, have you seen the article about Central State Hospital in the paper today?"

"No, I have not read the paper yet," Donna answered.

"Well, it is about the cemetery at the 'State' (name for mental hospital). It made me sad at first. Then, I realized something sort of scary."

"What is that?"

"Well, it's about my present mental condition . . . you know, if I had been born several decades ago, I probably would *not* be at home now. My family would have wanted to admit me to the 'State,' " I related.

"Wow, I guess you are probably right."

"Growing up in Georgia, I know you remember the familiar saying; if someone acted strange, they said, 'You are going to end up in Milledgeville.' (That saying was synonymous with the mental institution, originally called the State Lunatic Asylum. Of course, to most people the saying was considered humorous and everyone laughed.)

"Yes, I remember hearing that plus all the scary stories that went with it about shock treatment and padded cells."

"The article saddened me to think about all those people . . . so many of them tossed away by society. Medical science was still learning how to treat their mental infirmities so many of them never improved and died there."

"Well, luckily, the medical profession has come a long way since then."

"That is true."

"Don't worry, I am sure you are going to be all right."

A little later, my supervisor from work called to check on me. Also, she inquired about details concerning my job. At one point, she brought me a laptop computer to do some work. I don't remember doing any work; my mind could not handle anything.

The director could not understand what my issues were, or why I could not be at work although I had been under a doctor's care since September 15th. Someone said he thought I had abandoned my job. Of course, I was worried to death about my work there and being absent. But there was nothing I could do.

No one had ever seen me when I was in a deep depression. I always stayed home during these times, and kept to myself. I rarely ever told anyone what was going on with myself. Usually, I snapped out of it after a week or two, so I managed to "act" O.K that long.

So, my "new" demeanor was a total reversal for me. Everyone knew me as an outgoing, fun-loving, sociable person. No one had ever seen me without a smile on my face or joking about something. They could not imagine my being sad or upset.

My family called often, obviously very concerned about my condition.

"Marlene, are you feeling any better?" my mother asked.

"Mama, I still feel like I am having a nervous breakdown. I feel awful, and cannot stop crying." As I was talking, I was choking back the tears. We talked a little longer, and then hung up. By then, I was crying uncontrollably.

My friends knew something was wrong with me when I did not want to socialize; normally, I loved being with people. Constantly, my friends called, wanting to get me out of the house. My good friend from work, Pam, called, with her "Cheer up, things will get better . . . look on the bright side" attitude.

Believe me, I wanted to cheer up more than anything else.

Pam: "Marlene, I think if you went to lunch, you would feel better."

Me: "Pam, I cannot handle getting out."

Pam: "Gosh, what are you so down about? You have a good life, numerous friends, a good job, and the children are fine."

"I really don't know. That is what makes it so hard. I cry all the time. When I sleep, I wake up as tired as when I went to sleep. I feel horrible."

"I think if you get out, it will make you feel better."

"There is no way I can handle going anywhere. Going to lunch and pretending to act like 'life is O.K.' is just out of the question."

The thought of having to pretend everything was normal was unimaginable. Everything seemed overwhelming. I hated the way I felt, but I could not will myself to feel better. I guess I could not expect anyone to really understand my situation.

Just the thought of having to take a shower, get dressed, do something with my hair and face seemed totally exhausting. Normally, I did not leave the house without fixing myself up.

Many days I woke up and said to myself,

Today, I am going to feel better. But, every day I felt the same. I could not control or change my mental outlook. I truly hoped that it was a matter of making up my mind to feel better, or to think pos-

16

itively. But, in this case, it was not a matter of will. It was a much deeper matter.

Twenty-five years of rough times had worn me down. A series of traumatic events and illnesses had followed one after another. Stressful times turned into days, months, and years. The trauma, the stress, the enormous workload, the absence of my children—the combination had tipped the scales to the point that my mind and body could not handle any more.

What specific event had triggered my collapse? I did not know. But, I felt unstable, uninterested in anything and worn out.

Three
Strange Things

(When I started searching through my notes about this horrible time of my life, I found reminders of some interesting things . . . particularly, the spider web episode.) During this time while I was at home, I did a very peculiar thing. One day when I was sitting at the dining room table and looking out through the sliding glass door at the back yard, I noticed a large, almost perfect spider web. It was an amazingly large web, probably eighteen inches across. Part of it was attached to the eave, and the other part was attached to the sliding glass door.

Most people would have grabbed a broomstick and immediately knocked it down. Instead, I became obsessed with the preservation of this web. I don't know why I was so adamant about this web, but at the time it was an urgent and important matter. My thoughts were to preserve it by spraying it with clear acrylic paint and attach it on a board for a school science class. So, I wrote a note and taped it to the sliding glass door, "To everyone, please do not knock down the spider web. I am going to give it to a science class."

Someone should have sensed that something was wrong with me then. For my entire life, I have had a deadly fear of spiders. I do not remember now what happened to the web, but I do know that I never took it to a science class. The spider story was one of the weird obsessions I had; but, at the time, it seemed very normal to me.

Another unusual thing I did was to start walking with a wooden cane since my back was still bothering me. I collected old canes as a hobby, so I had a few to choose from. I tried out all of them. Eventually, I picked out a cane that seemed the easiest to use. I practiced walking inside first to get my balance. Then, I tried walking outside with it. Quickly, I found out how hard it was to balance and use a cane . . . especially, if the grass was damp. While I was practicing with it, I almost slipped down several times on the wet grass.

Very rarely did I actually leave the house . . . only to make a short trip to the quickie store to get milk or juice. When I *did* leave, I used the cane, even though I was very self-conscious and unsteady with it. It helped ease my back pain. Also, for some strange reason, I wanted people to see that something was wrong with me. I cannot explain why.

Thinking about that cane just reminded me of something else I did. On these quick trips to the convenience store, I started wearing a baseball cap to conceal my identity. My wearing a cap was very unusual, but I was ashamed of anyone seeing my unkempt hair. Did not have the energy to wash or style it. Large sunglasses hid my face, a bare face with no make-up. Part of me did not want anyone to see me, or recognize me, especially without make-up. Plus, I knew if I ran into a neighbor or friend, I could not explain why I was not working. No way to conceal my present mental situation . . . usually when I talked, I started crying.

Even simple things were a tremendous effort. Everything took a lot of energy: taking a shower, washing my hair and even going to the toilet. Our bathroom was small with the toilet paper roll dispenser located directly across on the opposite wall from the toilet. I lacked the energy to even hold up my head. So, when I used the toilet, I leaned forward and laid my head on the dispenser, even if I was only there a few minutes. I thought to myself, "Now, I know why they put the dispenser there; so, I can rest my head on it."

My daughter often came by the house to see me. She was in college and lived in an apartment in town. One afternoon, as we were talking, I told her about an incident that had happened when I went out for an errand. Several cars were turning into a car dealership at the busiest intersection on the main highway through our town. They were in front of me, and I noticed that they were causing a huge traffic jam. Determined to take the matter into my own hands, I threw my car into 'park' in the middle of the road, started honking the horn, and jumped out. I yelled, "Go on, you are going to cause a wreck," as I motioned for the cars to move on. Heads started bobbing around in the cars, and everyone started honking their horns simultaneously. I don't think most of them even knew why they were honking. The queue of cars lurched forward. For some reason, I thought it was hilarious.

I have no memory of Ash's reaction to my story. But, I imagine she thought it was strange for her mother to honk the horn, jump out of the car in the middle of a very busy highway, and start yelling at someone. Plus it was definitely a dangerous thing to do.

Four

Outpouring

Saturday, Sept. 27 (Conversation is from my journal.)
My husband had gone to run errands.

I was crying when he walked in the door.

"Why are you so sad?"

"I think I am suffering with depression . . . clinical depression."

"What exactly is that?"

I knew I could not talk about it without crying. So, I handed him a piece of paper on which I had scribbled down the symptoms that applied to me. I had actually numbered them as you see below:

1. No energy.
2. Constant, tired feeling; overwhelmed by anything (small or large).
3. Feeling of inadequacy; want to feel normal; cannot "will" myself to do so.
4. Want to work, go out, exercise, socialize; feel badly about myself because it is such a struggle to do so.
5. Unable to function in a normal way—want to have energy to cook, clean, take care of children, etc. Did cooking even when I've been feeling horrible. Needed to take care of myself, instead. Is difficult to take care of myself because I always think I need to take care of my children, and my work. I try to go to everything in hopes of

feeling better by getting out. I try to please everyone, but tend to not take care of myself.

6. Chemical imbalance. Something is wrong inside my head; my brain cannot emit the right amount of chemicals for me to function in a normal way.[1]

He sank down into a chair as he read my scribblings. "I had no idea what you were going through. You have never told me all of this."

"Oh, I just couldn't talk about it, and I did not want you to know."

"Well, lately, I have been trying to figure things out . . . like how can you talk and be fine one minute, and several hours later, be so different? You know . . . crying and depressed."

"I don't know myself. . . . I battle this depression every day. . . . Right now, I cannot stop crying. Then, sometimes, I feel well enough to keep going and function normally."

He seemed surprised. We had been married six years, but he had never seen me in this condition.

"I can't get over it. I just thought . . . you know . . . that you were O.K. This is the first time I have actually seen you this sad or act unusual in any way."

"To tell you the truth . . . (from my journal) I have been hiding these problems for years. As long as I wore my 'happy mask,' no one knew. Besides, the depression only lasted for a while, and then I felt better. No one needed to know."

"Gosh, you always seemed fairly happy."

"I have gotten very good at *acting* like I am O.K. I have done it for so long that it has become part of me."

"So, what do you think has happened now?"

"I don't know exactly. I can no longer hide my feelings, or my emotions . . . everything is coming out . . . whether I want it to or not. Sadness, anger, frustration . . . I cannot control them. I

22

don't know what to do, but I am afraid of the intense feelings I am having. Anyway, right now, I am so tired . . . I need to go to bed."

I do not know how that conversation ended. My mind and body were both bone tired . . . aching with weariness.

I did not have the energy to explain what was tumbling around in my head.

Horrible, bad thoughts had captivated me. Many bad experiences had taken over my mind; started dwelling on getting even with people who had disappointed me. Was going to let them have it. . . . I did not mean physical violence . . . just tell them off . . . let them know how they had hurt me. Insecurities from my past were yelling at me now. Past hurts deeply buried resurfaced with a vengeance. Felt wounded with even more intensity.

(From my jottings.) . . . I went to bed about 10:30 P.M. and slept for a few hours. I woke up because my legs were twitching, and I could not keep them still. I tried hard to stop my legs from moving, but it was impossible to stay still. Felt very agitated. Same reaction I have had before with certain decongestants and sinus medicines. Plus, my back was still hurting.

Sunday, Sept. 28

(From my notes.) This was not a case of the blues . . . it was much worse. I felt so helpless and hopeless. I had hit rock bottom. The best way to describe it was I felt like I was in a dark place; a deep, dark pit with no escape. I wanted to climb out of this place. Everything seemed overwhelming and frustrating and dark. I just wanted to stop the horror as soon as I could. I knew I could not take it much longer. Apparently, the anti-depressant, Serzone, was not working for me. It was like taking a sugar pill—nothing ever happened.

Probably around 8:00 or 9:00 P.M. I went into our bedroom, and closed the bedroom door. Crying, out of control . . . felt the veins bulging on my forehead. Felt empty . . . So afraid but had reached my wits' end . . . dialed my physician in Macon (35 miles away) . . . he had treated me for depression after Ty was born. If I can just get a message to him . . . he will understand. When I finally reached the doctor's answering service, they were no help . . . very frustrating. Mind, racing out of control. Crying uncontrollably . . . finally, found Crisis Line in Macon phone book. I was shaking as I dialed.

"Crisis Line, this is Dennis."

"I am extremely depressed," I sobbed, "I have been feeling suicidal . . . I think I am having a nervous breakdown," I whispered, barely able to get the words out.

Up until this point, I had not told anyone how I really felt. I hated to admit that, 'Suicide seemed like the best way to escape the pain and mental agony.'

I was a Christian, and Christians should not be depressed. A true Christian certainly would not even consider suicide as a choice. That mode of thinking only made me feel worse.

Dennis was warm and comforting, but I cannot remember what he said, exactly. Something to the effect of, "I am going to take care of you. I will get you help as soon as possible."

"Thanks . . . I know I need it (help). Monday night and tonight I've been on the verge of suicide."

"Listen, it is O.K., I will help you. Do you want to tell me your name?"

"Yes, my name is Marlene _____."

We talked on for several minutes.

"Can you make it through the night, or do you need treatment now?" He seemed so kind.

At last, someone who seemed to understand my terrible state of mind; who validated the fact that I was a person in a crisis situation.

"I believe I will be O.K. tonight."

"Fine, I will give you a physician to call and make an appointment. Just explain what you have told me, and he will set up an appointment as soon as possible."

"Thank you very much."

"I am glad to help. Also, there is something else you can do. You can get a free consultation at the psychiatric hospital in Macon. Let me give you that phone number."

"O.K."

"So, are you sure that you are all right tonight?"

"Yes, I am O.K."

He ended with, "Now, call me back if you need to."

I promised I would.

I felt very relieved that I had taken that step—to call for help. But, I was very afraid about what was happening to me.

I felt sad, dark, empty What if I am going crazy?

Then, there was a knock on my bedroom door. It was my husband. When he came in, he just looked at me, and said,"I just don't understand what has happened to you. Why are you so upset and stressed out?"

"Well, I really don't know what has happened to me, but I just called Crisis Line for help. I need to go to a psychiatric hospital as soon as possible. But, I am so afraid to go."

"Oh, O.K.," he responded. I saw no emotion, but his face seemed strained. (I was sorry I was in this terrible state, but I could not help it.)

"I need to see a psychiatrist as soon as possible . . . and, I really need you to go with me."

He agreed.

I cannot remember any more.

Five

Help

Monday, September 29, 9:00 A.M.

I set up an appointment for a free consult for 7:00 P.M. that same evening. Naturally, my husband was having an extremely hard time understanding what had caused the change in me. I am sure he thought I should just stop sleeping and crying all the time and just go back to work. He could not possibly fathom what was happening to me nor understand my mental agony. I hoped that the consult would clarify things for both of us.

That afternoon we headed to the hospital for our appointment. Needless to say, the thirty-five-minute drive was awful. I could have cut the tension with a knife. Neither one of us said a word . . . not one word. Looking back I imagine he was probably trying to figure how to escape the whole situation. I was wondering what was wrong with me.

We arrived at the hospital, and within a few minutes we were called into an office. A young lady asked me the usual information. Name, address, illnesses, and on and on.

Then, she asked, "Why are you here?"

"I am very depressed and worried because I seem to be getting worse."

"Are you suicidal?"

"No, not right now . . . I am O.K., at the moment. I was suicidal before."

"What stopped you from commiting suicide?"

"I don't know . . . I kept thinking about the people who loved me and needed me."

"What medications are you taking now?"

"I am taking Serzone, Estrogen, and Ambien (for sleep)."

We asked some questions, and the conversation ended, as far as I could remember.

I wish I could remember more about our visit, but my mental state was so shaky. Thank heavens, I was coherent enough to know something was wrong with me, and I had the presence of mind to record most of my experiences and scribble down notes. My actual memory from that period of time is mostly a blur.

We returned home in silence. It seemed like it was a total waste of time.

Tuesday, September 30

The next morning I took the counselor's advice and called to make an appointment with a psychiatrist. I had been to a psychiatrist before for various problems; but, things were very different this time. My mind had never been racing out of control. Very scary. *What would he do to me?*

I was able to get an appointment in about a week. To me that seven days was an eternity.

Called the local psychiatrist to get an appointment sooner. His next available appointment two weeks away . . . no way I could wait that long. Kept appointment, for one week.

Called back to my first appointment in Macon.

"Hello, I just made an appointment a little while ago. But, I am having so much trouble sleeping. Could anyone else see me any sooner?"

"No, not really. We are booked full. Actually . . . huh . . . never mind. . . ."

"What is it? I asked.

27

"I probably should not tell you this, but to be completely honest . . . you could have gotten immediate attention."

"What do you mean?"

"When you went to the 'consult' last night at the Psychiatric Hospital, did the clerk ask if you were suicidal?"

"Yeah."

"If you had answered, 'Yes, I am suicidal,' they would have admitted you immediately."

"But, I did not *feel* suicidal at that moment. Plus, I really do not want to go into a mental facility."

We talked on a few minutes until I heard a click of a key at the side door. It was my wonderful daughter, Ashley. She had come by to check on me between her college classes. What a special daughter! Plus, she brought me four or five copies of my article I had written in a local magazine for senior citizens.[1] I was very glad to see it in print, and always happy to see her.

Wednesday, Oct. 1, 10:00 A.M.

Doctor appointment with Dr Dillon. Prescribed Ambien (10 mg.) to help me sleep. Also, I asked him to send a letter addressing certain issues to the Library Director.

Here is the letter:

Dear Jim Roberts:

I have been treating Marlene—for fibromyalgia and and an associated condition, depression. She has been in a severe state of depression during the past few weeks.

The enclosure from Coliseum Psychiatric Hospital states that Marlene had an assessment evaluation on Monday, September 30, 1997, at 7:00 P.M. Her husband accompanied her.

The enclosure from Center for Psychiatric Hospital states that Marlene has an appointment with Kara Bench R.N.C.S., and Dr. William Simmons on October 8, 1997. They will evaluate/change/monitor her medication for depression. They, also, will set up counseling sessions for Marlene and her husband.

28

Marlene has the conscientious desire to work as she has continued to communicate daily about the government document work with her supervisor, Nancy Bray.

Due to Marlene's physical condition, she cannot work at this time. She needs rest, as her body adapts to new medication. She cannot handle even the smallest amount of stress.

Marlene and her husband have a trip planned to go to the mountains, October 10–12. Although she has depleted her annual and sick leave, and is now receiving sick hours from the "sick leave pool," this trip would be beneficial for her health. If she is back to work by then, she would need to take at least four hours leave on Friday, October 10, 1997. Your consideration in granting this time could possibly speed up her recovery.

Sincerely,

Roger Dillon, M.D.[2]

Six
Earlier Manifestations

As I mentioned previously, this episode was not my first bout of depression. Actually, going way back, I had experienced periods of sadness in high school. At that time, I really did not know what it was, and I never talked to anyone about it. Maybe, the sadness lasted about a week and then went away.

In college I experienced crying spells and sadness, but did not think it was an unusual situation. I considered the sad times as relating to the stress of college life—the usual grades, tests, dating, the future.

I recalled a conversation at that time with a college friend who had gone home one weekend. She ran into an old friend in her hometown who began to talk about some of the same things I was feeling. The friend said she felt very sad and dark on the inside; that her whole body felt completely black within, and she did not know what to do about it. I knew exactly what she was experiencing.

Later on, I asked my friend, "Did you ever talk again with your friend who seemed depressed?"

"Uh, no, not really."

"Gosh, I wonder what happened to her."

"Well, actually, I did hear, but I did not want to tell you."

"Why?"

"She eventually commited suicide, and I thought it would upset you."

"Gosh, I hate that. I wonder why she did it."

I heard she said, "She could no longer stand the darkness."

I was sad, although I did not even know the girl.

As time passed I began to go into deeper depressions. Hopelessness and helplessness were very prevalent. I remember feeling dark on the inside, down in a deep pit. Maybe, this was the darkness the girl had experienced. These episodes lasted from two to three weeks.

Another college friend directed me to a wonderful psychotherapist, who had helped her mother and sister through episodes of deep depression. As I mentioned earlier, these depressions seemed connected to marital problems, health issues and surgeries.

Although these therapeutic sessions were difficult, together we explored my past, and she gave me positive strategies to work on my self-esteem, and my guilt. With antidepressants, prayer, coping strategies and time, I dealt with the depressive periods.

Seven

The Switch

But never had I experienced anything that hung on this long with no relief. The antidepressant, Serzone, never seemed to make any difference. I just went further and further down . . . like being sucked down into a drain.

Thursday, October 2

Went to bed about 10:15 or so. Fantastic night's sleep. Best sleep in who knows went (when). Did not wake up until the phone rang . . . it was Mama. Felt so drowsy, and eyelids so heavy . . . I could have slept forever . . . almost impossible to keep my eyes open. Had already slept about twelve hours.

After I hung up the phone with Mama, I dragged myself out of bed. Began a flurry of writing . . . Wrote down every medicine I was taking, the exact dosage, times I took them . . . very worried about my memory . . . becoming obsessed with writing everything down . . . every single thing that I need to do, everything I need to think about, and mark it after I have done it. Every item is numbered, in order.

Friday–Sunday, Oct. 3–5

Things started changing; the darkness lifted, and my mind raced. I began to have tons of energy, and I cleaned for hours without getting tired. One day I spent extremely long hours cleaning, and reorganizing drawers. I did not get tired.

The main thing that bothered me was that I had problems organizing my thoughts. I was trying to compose a letter to a couple whose house we were hoping to buy. As I cleaned, I was working on the letter in my head. Then, I stopped to write it on paper. I cleaned and composed; cleaned and composed for *ten* straight hours.

That simple task of writing a letter seemed to take on a tremendous importance. I had to use the perfect words, and I felt our successful purchase depended on the wording of my letter. All the pressure was on me and I could not fail! Concentrating was extremely hard; and, keeping my mind on the task was a huge obstacle. I checked the dictionary dozens of times for more appropriate words. I could **not** fail! The letter took me the entire ten hours to get it absolutely perfect.

Ordinary things seemed like brilliant ideas. I started going through all the files in my filing cabinets. Each label represented a topic that was special, such as, "favorite celebrities," "authors," or "unusual stories." I viewed things with perfect clarity. My amazing thought was that: *Someone can just go through my filing cabinet and write my life's story. All the things that are important to me are in those files; it would be easy for someone to write about me.* That idea seemed fantastic . . . that someone would be enthralled with my everyday topics and want to write a book about me.

My mind continued to race at lightning speed, and ideas poured out. Rapid speech. My nerves were still on edge . . . I was very agitated and irritated with everything and everybody. Still the nagging chest pains . . . probably, just stress. Thought of funny stories. In fact, everything was absolutely hilarious, and I started making up comical dialogues about neighbors and people I knew. I laughed out loud as the words came pouring out at a rapid pace. I could not say the words fast enough to keep up with my mind. I talked, laughed and recorded them on tape.

No one ever saw me or heard me during these taping sessions.

However, ten years later I am still searching for those tapes. Guess I must have accidentally taped over them.

My mind was out of control. I began to get very weary, but I could not stop my mind from racing. I was bone-tired, and would get ready for bed. I laid down, closed my eyes, but I could not sleep. My mind raced endlessly. So, I got up without waking my husband and headed to the kitchen and den.

I did whatever household chores needed to be done; I was a person who hated to waste my time. At all hours of the night until early morning I washed clothes, unloaded the dishwasher, paid bills or dusted the house. I channeled my energy. I was getting more and more tired, but my mind would not slow down. It was miserable. Of course, I could not return to work like this.

During this time, the pacing began . . . all night long. I went into the laundry room, sorted the clothes for a few minutes, and the next thing I knew I was back in the big den walking up and down the room. This pattern continued with whatever chore I tried to do. I started on a task, then stopped, went into the den where there was more room, and starting pacing up and down the floor like a caged animal. After a few minutes, I went back to the task. The pacing continued until I finally got tired enough to go to sleep again. Sometimes, it might be 4:00 or 5:00 in the morning.

Also, the hair pulling began. As I was pacing, I remembered running my fingers through my scalp and hair obsessively. Then, I grabbed my hair by the roots with both hands. I began doing this over and over . . . running my fingers through my scalp and pulling my hair. It actually felt pretty good. I don't think I ever tugged hard enough to pull any hair out. I thought about the expression, 'someone wanting to pull their hair out.' Now, I literally knew what they meant. Did this expression start with someone in my condition?

At the same time my low moan whispering "Oh . . . oh . . . oh" started. This new pattern began with whatever task I tried to do. I started on a task, then stopped, started pacing the floor, pull-

34

ing my hair, and moaning. After a little while I returned to the task. In spite of my unusual rituals, I actually *was* able to get a lot of things accomplished.

Of course, I don't believe anyone ever saw me pacing or pulling my hair . . . or heard my moaning. And, I never told a soul about it . . . not even my husband. Why did I keep it a secret? Maybe, I did not think it was unusual at the time.

Monday, October 6

Received a call from psychiatrist in Macon that I would see the clinical nurse specialist as well as the psychiatrist on October 8. She said the assessment was usually ninety minutes. Then, this specialist shared the information with the doctor. He would prescribe medicine if necessary. Good, at least, I feel like something was being accomplished.

Returned to general physician (Dr. Dillon) for refills on Serzone and Ambien. Still having back pain.

He sent me to another doctor without an appointment.

4:10 P.M. Drove to doctor's office, and walked in. Headed straight to the front desk.

"May I help you?" the receptionist inquired.

"Listen, I *have* to see the doctor," I demanded.

"Have you seen him before?"

"No," I snapped back. Heads began to turn among the ladies behind the counter.

"You will have to fill out some paperwork, then."

"O.K., I will try to . . . if I can concentrate." All their eyes were on me now.

"What is your problem exactly?" she asked.

"Look, I can't talk about it. I just need help," I growled.

"O.K., we will see what we can do."

I walked over to the chairs to sit down. The ladies glanced toward me and started whispering immediately.

I knew they were talking about me, but I did not care. Very agitated. Could not sit still. Started pacing up and down the reception area. I don't know if there were other patients there or not. The ladies watched every move I made.

Then, the doctor called me back.

"Hello, Marlene, what can I do for you?" (I knew him.)

"Well, I am having a lot of problems, but I think I have some sort of kidney or bladder trouble; that is the reason I came to see you. Dr. Dillon sent me," I explained. I elaborated on my problems.

"In light of everything that is going on with you, what would you like for me to do? I can admit you to the hospital or treat you as an outpatient," he calmly said.

"I guess as an outpatient."

"O.K., well it seems you do have a kidney infection which we will treat. Most likely that is the reason for your back pain."

"Thank you very much. You have been great."

(From notes.) "That Stacy (receptionist at the doctor's office) has some sort of problem; she is not accommodating for people in severe crisis. Hopefully, her personality will appear different to me when I feel better. I wonder if she is the one who was so rude when I called. It will be interesting to find out at a later date."

Good, so my back pain was not my imagination, after all. After using the medicine for several days, my pain began to lessen. After a week's usage the cane became optional and within a few weeks, I completely stopped using it.

Still a few chest pains during the night.

Eight
The Shrink

Wednesday, October 8

The day finally arrived for my first appointment . . . my first visit to "Center for Psychiatric Care."

(It is very difficult to recall a lot of the details during those months, but I do remember this office visit to the doctor.)

My sister Dianne had driven down to take me to the appointment. Before she arrived, I had become obsessed with compiling all the pharmacy receipts, bills of all doctors' visits, and hospital stays for my entire life. I felt I could not go without taking this huge box of papers with me. Also, I felt compelled to have everything in chronological order. At the time, it seemed absolutely necessary.

(Dianne's memory of the situation.) Our family did not realize that Marlene had been out of work, and at home, crying, and sleeping most of the time, for several weeks. She called me to ask if I could take her to the doctor in Macon. During our conversation she mentioned she had been gathering stacks of records and files for her visit. Well, I had no idea until I arrived.

I had taken off work to drive down. She answered the door and was very hyper-active, flitting from one thing to another. I had never seen her in this condition and was shocked at her behavior. She was frantically stuffing papers into files, and organizing them in a large cardboard box along with supplies of pens, pencils, glue, and scissors. She said she absolutely *had* to get them in date order. Suddenly, she remembered she had not eaten lunch so she rushed into the kitchen to microwave her plate of vegetables.

Her attention span was extremely short. She left her lunch and came back into the den quickly gathering several large Ziploc baggies packed full of empty medicine bottles.

I inquired about them, and she said the doctor could tell exactly what she had taken and when. Then, she headed back to the kitchen to microwave her plate of food again.

Finally, I got all of her boxes, papers, and records into the car. As we drove toward Macon, she started talking about a lot of things that happened growing up, how she felt about certain upsetting situations. Then, her mind would revert back to her task, and she would say, "Dianne, I have to get everything in order."

She would work a few minutes, and then she would start rambling about her childhood, emphasizing what she was going to say to those who had wronged her. She continued this behavior for the entire forty-five minute trip.

I was thinking to myself, *Oh, my goodness . . . what am I going to do? I was an absolute nervous wreck, but I had to be strong. I will try to go along with what she wants so we can get through the situation. Even though I was very stressed out, she did not realize it. There Marlene was . . . she wanted to eat her lunch in the car, but did not have a fork. It was easy to tell . . . she was not her normal self.*

We finally arrived at the office where I hauled in her box packed with information and bags of medicine bottles. We checked in and sat down in the waiting room. She started trying to fill out the paperwork. Then, she stopped, looked at me, and began to cry.

"Marlene, what is wrong?"

"I want to write down today's date, but I cannot remember what it is. I don't even know the month or year," she said, choking back the tears.

She could not remember numbers or anything, and she kept crying for a while.

I assured her that it was O.K., and that I would help her.

After we finished, and took the paperwork and insurance cards to the receptionist, Marlene began unpacking the box. She began taking all the stacks of receipts, prescriptions, and papers, and spreading them all in stacks on the floor around her chair. She was obsessed with having them organized.

She started handing me medicine bottles and asking,

"Dianne, when did I start taking this? What's the date? When did I stop?" I was trying my dead level best to help her. "I need to know this; now, read through this and tell me what it says," she continued.

Then, she said, "I have *got* to have a paper clip."

So, I went to the receptionist, and said, "My sister *really* wants some paper clips. Would you please give me some? As you can see, she is having some problems."

The receptionist nodded in agreement and gave them to me. Other patients, along with their relatives and friends, watched as she shuffled papers and bags of medicines. She was undeterred, and continued the maddening pace until she was called back for her appointment. I stayed in the waiting room, trying to remain calm.

(Marlene speaking.) Finally, my name was called. Kara, the clinical nurse specialist, met me at the doorway, shook my hand, and guided me back to her office. She was kind, but very straight-forward with me. I could hardly speak for crying every few minutes.

Kara explained, "Marlene, I will counsel you, and then I will discuss my findings with the doctor, (who is a licensed psychiatrist). Then, he will prescribe the appropriate medicine, if necessary."

39

"Is it permissible for me to record these sessions?" I asked. "I want my husband to hear them."

"Sure, it is fine with me. Now, tell me how you are doing."

"Well, I am in a terrible depression. For several days in September, I felt suicidal."

"What about today?"

"I do not feel suicidal today; I am still very depressed, in one sense. But my mind is racing, and I can't sleep."

"O.K., can you tell me about your medical history? Number of children . . . surgeries, that sort of thing."

"In 1976, my daughter was born; in 1982 I had a miscarriage; then my son was born in 1983. He had some serious health problems which overwhelmed me." I continued on and on without stopping . . . about my years of depression, sleepless nights, walking the floors and praying for the answers for my son's life.

She had to stop me and get me back on track. Our session had already lasted probably twenty to twenty-five minutes by now.

"O.K., we have enough history for now so let me get some copies of your paperwork, and get Dr. Simmons to come on in. I will be right back."

(A few minutes later.) "What about any medications you are taking?"

"Well, my doctor recently switched me from Elavil and Effexor (for depression) to Serzone. I asked him to do it since I did not think those medicines were helping."

"When you say 'doctor,' what type of doctor?"

"He is a general medical physician."

"How much of each medicine were you taking?"

By now, Dr. Simmons entered the room. He was a good-looking man with a gentle voice; he immediately said hello and reached forward to shake my hand.

"Uh, I don't know exactly how much I was taking. My mind was a complete blank on this. I think I have it written down, somewhere." (I felt so silly not knowing how much medicine I had been taking, and nervously fumbled through my stack of papers, and my briefcase. I was sweating profusely now.) I finally located the amounts.

"Have you had any blood work done recently?" Dr. Simmons inquired.

"No, not lately."

He seemed bothered that a physician had not recently ordered any blood work for me.

Then, I started trying to tell him a lot of information about my situation and depression. I talked on and on. He finally was able to stop me from my nonstop soliloquy. (I did not know I was talking so much until I played back the tapes from these sessions.)

After several more questions, he related, "Marlene, from what you are telling me, I know what you have, and we can help you."

What wonderful words! What a huge relief . . . my problem has a name and he can help me! I cannot believe it.

"Your symptoms indicate you have a 'mood affective disorder,' called 'bipolar disorder.' It used to be called 'manic depression.' The good news is we have very effective medications to manage it now." He spoke in a warm, reassuring manner, and I immediately liked him.

"Thanks . . . thank you so much."

"Most likely, we will start you on an antidepressant for your depression, and then Depacote to help with the mood swings. Depacote is used instead of Lithium which was used in the past. The advantage of Depacote is that the dosages can be regulated much easier. O.K., Marlene, here is what we need for you to do:

"Continue to take one tablet of Serzone after supper. Take your Ambien, as prescribed, for sleep.

"Get an EKG plus blood and lab work done tomorrow at your local hospital. Have them fax the results of the EKG and all the lab work immediately to us. We cannot prescribe any additional medicine until we get all of your bloodwork and results. That is why it

41

all needs to be done immediately. Do you understand everything so far?"

"I am a little overwhelmed, but I think so."

"Meanwhile, we need all the information on psychiatrists you have seen previously. Also, a list of prescription medicines you have taken in the past. I want to see you again in one week."

He was kind, yet informative. His manner put me at ease for the first time in a long time. He realized I was in a crisis mode and needed help as soon as possible. Although the session was hard for me emotionally, I felt a great sense of relief.

(Dianne again.) When Marlene came out after her session, we gathered everything up, and walked outside.

She immediately started bawling, and said, "Dianne, I have finally found *someone . . . someone* who can help me."

I wanted to break down and cry with her. But, I felt like I had to hold things together. I did not know if we would get home or not; the whole situation had just torn me out of the frame. To be honest, I was disgusted and disillusioned about bringing her back home. I really felt like the doctor should have convinced her to enter the mental hospital immediately. She was very unstable. I did not feel good about leaving her at home in the condition she was in, but I did not know what to do. She seemed O.K. about going back home.

Later, another thought hit me. I remembered that Marlene had bought a handgun several years before. She was worried about protecting the children when her husband went out of town. She had taken all the precautions of getting her firearms license, learning gun safety, and taking target practice. Was her loaded gun still in the drawer of the nightstand by her bed? Or, had her husband hidden it?

(Marlene.) That night . . . slept from 10:00–11:30 P.M. Woke up with chest pains; maybe, sleeping in an uncomfortable way;

have had chest pains in past three to four nights. When first woke up, felt like a twinge of pain toward my left breast . . . as if heart was racing and compressing at the same time . . . possibly beating too fast? Did not tell my husband (what else is new?). Will worry him/already worried enough. Had trouble sleeping because of pain, stayed up all night. Finally, fell back to sleep about 5:00 A.M.

Nine

More Panic Attacks

Thursday, October 9, 1997
(Very detailed chart of medicines, times taken.)

My mind is racing one hundred miles an hour, but I am getting very slow in doing many things because I have to conscientiously think about every little thing. Took me about forty-five minutes to eat lunch. Needed to call the psychiatrist but had to collect my thoughts before I could make the call . . . had to write down *everything*.

Even reading is becoming difficult . . . hard to describe exactly. I look at the words on a page, but my mind is running ahead of the words. I cannot slow my mind down . . . don't understand what the words mean. I hate this! What am I going to do?

My daily reminder List:

Suppertime: Take 1 tablet of Serzone. (I checked it off when I took it.)

Need to take:

1. Take 1 tablet of Ambien for sleep. Maybe, I should wait to see if Dr. Simmons calls.
2. Call Cathy back (only if I can think about it first). Tell her about possible diagnosis of bipolar disorder/manic

44

depression . . . can be treated with medication. Tell her we wish Sara (her daughter) good luck on Homecoming Court, and to take pictures.

3. Ash may come after 8:00 P.M.; may eat with us.
4. When phone rings, let message machine answer it. Maybe, return Janet's call, if feel like it. She wished us a good trip.
5. May return Pam's call, if able; she has to work on Friday.
6. Dry the clothes.
7. Take bath/wash hair.

This detailed and extensive list became a daily regimen for me. Each day I made out a list. It was pitiful to think that I had to write down even the simplest things . . . what I needed to say or do. Had to think about phone calls before I made them so I could write down whatever I wanted to tell them . . . otherwise, I might not remember. Also, my calling depended on if I had the energy to make the calls.

Not to mention, my poor memory was getting dangerous. I had gotten to the point that I could not remember if I just took a pill, or if I still needed to take it. For the type of medicine I was taking, it could be disastrous. I hated this state of mind . . . being out of control and not knowing what to do next.

(Same night.) 8:00 P.M. My husband and I eating supper, and watching TV. I felt calm. Ash did not come to eat with us.

Then, the tightness started, a severe pain in chest, felt like [heart] couldn't beat, fingertips felt like they were asleep. . . . Told husband, he assured me it was stress. Got more and more scared.

"I am having a heart attack," I gasped.

"No, it is just stress."

"What should I do, what should I do?"

"Calm down, you will be O.K.," he assured.

"Should I sit up, or lie down? I really think I am having a heart attack, it really hurts." (felt as if I might die.) [sic]

"You are O.K."

"How do you know that? Well, I guess if I am having an attack, I will die right here. Then you will say, 'I guess it was real,' " I argued.

We continued to argue about it.

"Just stay where you are."

"I don't want to die, I don't want to die," I sobbed.

The stabbing pain continued for a while, maybe twenty-five minutes . . . but I have no idea exactly how long. I felt drained and light-headed, but otherwise, O.K.

8:35 P.M. Dr. Simmons called. I was very surprised that a doctor would call me so late at home.

"Marlene, how are you?"

"Not good . . . I have just had some sort of episode with my heart aching, chest pains, and lightheadedness. I thought I was having a heart attack."

"Hmmm, sounds like a panic or anxiety attack."

"Well, I felt fairly calm before it began."

"These panic attacks can happen at any time. I will talk to you in more detail about these later. Actually, one of the medications I am prescribing should help with those attacks. Also, we will do some tests on your heart."

"Good, anything to help with these attacks."

"O.K. We have received the results of your blood work and EKG. Everything checks out so we can start your medications immediately. I do need to talk to whoever can go to the drugstore for you."

Do not remember much else about the conversation; the entire situation had become overwhelming for me.

Ash walked in while he and I were talking. I put her on the line so he could explain everything to her. She asked me which drugstore so he could call it in before 9:00 P.M. By now it was almost 8:45 P.M. I was pacing the floor by now . . . wringing my hands . . . so nervous that the store would close before she arrived. She hung up the phone and took off for the drugstore.

She returned with the medicine within fifteen minutes or so. We sat down, with the bag of prescriptions.

"Ash, I need you to help me. I cannot read and comprehend exactly what I need to do."

"Mama, don't worry."

She read the directions of each kind of medicine. Dr. Simmons prescribed Effexor for depression, Depacote for mood swings, and Klonopin (antiseizure) for anxiety or panic attacks. Ash gave me each pill. Then, she wrote down exactly what I had taken, and when I could take more of a certain pill. She stayed a while; I don't know how long.

Then, for some strange reason, I called my husband's parents. I talked to my father-in-law, and asked him if he could come pick me up. He seemed very surprised. (Normally, I rarely called them.) And, he told me that he felt that I needed to stay home. All I could think about was . . . their spacious, quiet house. I told him that I just wanted to go upstairs to a quiet bedroom and sleep. I was not at all worried about what he was thinking. We talked a few minutes, and he said it was best that I stay home. I don't think I even mentioned the conversation to my husband.

Later, I wrote a brief note about this night: '***Horrible*** night in *crisis.*' Thank you, Lord, that you helped me make it through. Help of my family and my doctor.

Friday, October 10

Slept really well last night. Did wake up with night sweats. Have not done that since the last two weeks of September.

My list today:

Morning:

Write down medicines and times to take them.

Pack clothes for mountain trip.

Call doctor about refill on medicines.

4:00 P.M. My husband and I left to go to North Carolina to the mountains. The doctors thought the change and rest would do me good. I was looking forward to this trip.

The drive up was fine. I felt O.K.

But my mind seems blank, and body feels numb to everything. Not happy or sad, just empty and blah. A grayish mood. I hate feeling "numb" . . . Sometimes it's worse than feeling bad. The nothingness . . . the emptiness is scary. I just trudge through the day on faith . . . I know God is with me . . . whether I feel it, or not. . . . He will see me through . . . somehow . . . faith is stretched thin now. . . . He seems so far away.

Reservations were at a very plain bed and breakfast in a quaint little town . . . which was basically a cabin with no TV or phone. Peace and quiet seemed like a great idea to me. I had not mentioned to my husband about no TV, and he was not happy about it.

We had dinner out. Returned to the cabin. Don't remember any other details. Went to sleep.

2:00 A.M. Woke up, sharp pain in chest, first felt like a hunger pang, then felt dizzy, nauseated, profuse sweating, felt weak. I stumbled to the bathroom. The next thing I remember was yelling for my husband. I don't know how much time had passed. He found me sitting against the wall in the bathroom. I remember his picking me up and putting me in bed. Felt feverish.

Saturday, October 11

8:00 A.M. Got up, felt sharp twinge of pain, left breast, under rib cage. Is this another anxiety attack? Took one tablet of Klonopin. (Used for anxiety and panic attacks.) Very puzzled

48

about these attacks because I am not upset or anxious when I have them. I seem to be very calm, but I cannot seem to control them.

During day, felt O.K. We went into cute shops and ate lunch at a good restaurant. Wanted to do more shopping, but absolutely exhausted.

Sunday, Oct. 12

No more details written. Returned home. Still, felt sort of gray.

Monday, Oct. 13

I was proud of myself for not crying all day long.

My good friend Cathy called; she reminded me I had not called my doctor this past Friday. It had slipped my mind. My memory is getting worse.

Since I had forgotten to call, the clinical nurse specialist called me first, and talked at length about my condition.

"So, how did you feel over the weekend?" Kara asked.

"Well, I continued to have the panic attacks fairly often . . . two or three times a day and at night."

"O.K., here is what you should do when the symptoms begin. Put one half tablet of Klonopin under your tongue, and let it melt; then swallow the other half. This method is the quickest way for the medicine to get into your system."

"What causes these attacks?"

"That is a good question. Many things can initiate an attack, and no one can predict when one may occur, or why," she explained. "Most likely, it is a combination of things . . . a chemical imbalance plus other issues which we will explore in counseling.

"Also, I wanted you to know we were able to get you in sooner to see Doctor Simmons because of your unstable condition. So, your initial visit was designated as a 'Crisis Intervention' visit."

"Thank for getting me in, I surely needed it."

49

"Our goal is to get you on an even keel. When you came in last week, your thoughts were scattered, your mind was in super speed, and you were headed toward the psychotic state. You had gone from extreme depression to the manic depressive phase. Actually, you were in the 'rapid cycling' mode, which meant your depression had switched rapidly to mania; from very low to very high. You were heading toward absolute confusion and psychosis," she explained.

All I know is that "I was very afraid of what was happening to me."

"I know you were. Dr. Simmons had to be sure your blood work from the lab was good, and that the EKG checked out O.K. for your heart. Until he had those results, he could not prescribe the specific medicines for you. But, he truly believes that the Effexor will be very good for your depression and the Depacote should regulate your mood swings."

"Good, I hope so."

"Of course, it will take some time for the medicine to take effect. Our goal is to get your mood balanced."

"O.K."

"Also, you can bring your husband or whoever you wish to your next appointment. We will all work together on this . . . so, don't worry," she said.

"Another problem is the financial part; I have good insurance, but they will not pay for certain things," I said.

"Don't worry, we will sit down and work out those details, too. Now, what other questions do you have?"

"I guess that is all I can think of. Thank you your help . . . and for calling me."

"If you have other problems, give us a call. Otherwise, I will see you on Thursday."

I hung up the phone. I could not get over the fact my clinical nurse specialist, Kara had called me, and that we had spent so much time on the phone.

50

7:30 P.M. Felt tightness in chest again. Dizzy. Realized was the onset of a panic attack so put the one half tablet under my tongue, and let it melt. After a little while, I felt O.K.

8:30 P.M. Started crying again. (Almost made it through the day without crying.)

Hard to remember anything. Have to write down every move. Even talk to myself out loud . . . to tell myself what to do next. Very sad! I know I need to be in a hospital for someone to administer my medicine, but I DO NOT WANT TO GO INTO THE HOSPITAL! (Do I make myself clear?)

Wednesday, Oct. 15

Went to my friend Janet's house for a short visit. As we were talking, felt pain in upper left breast, under my rib cage, dizzy, lightheaded, pain in chest. Immediately, left and took Klonopin on the way home. After an hour, still felt weak and dizzy.

(No other notes for that day.)

Ten

Second Shrink Visit

Thursday, Oct. 16

Around 10:30 A.M. had panic attack, took medicine.

Got call from Supervisor at work about my sick leave form. Upset about constant pressure from director verifying my sick leave status plus continual proof of why I am absent. Apparently, he did not believe I was really sick because he told someone I had "abandoned" my job; I could not believe it. I am one of the hardest workers they have. Went to library (my workplace), crying . . . having to tend to all these details when I feel so horrible. At work, I had always jokingly said, "If you are going to die, you have to give two weeks notice."

My original plan today was to go to the doctor, and then spend a week at my parents' house since my husband was going out of town. My sister Marilyn was driving down from Douglasville to take me to my doctor's appointment.

(Marilyn's memory of the day.) Before I went to Milledgeville to pick up Marlene for her second appointment with the psychiatrist, I had talked in depth with my sister Dianne, who had taken her to the first appointment the week before.

Dianne had explained the procedure about the visit—the clinical nurse specialist would talk with Marlene, or both of us first, relay the information to the doctor, and then he would come in.

When I arrived at Marlene's house, she was very busy getting all of her stuff together—I mean, ALL OF IT!!! Clothes plus a box of notebooks, books, glue, scissors, markers, and pencils. I knew she was planning to go to our parents' house for a week after this visit, but she was carrying almost everything she owned.

"Uh, do you think you need all of this?" I asked.

"Well, I have a lot of catching up on things I need to do; I don't really know what I will need so I am just taking everything."

"O.K.," I agreed.

After we loaded my Toyota Camry, it was bursting at the seams.

Marlene was quite chatty on the way to the doctor and seemed excited about this visit.

"I am so relieved I have a good doctor. I know he can help me."

"Yes, I want to meet him."

"My thing is I just can't cope with going into a mental facility."

"Why is that?"

"Well, I don't know what they would do to me. The thought of them tying me down and giving me shock treatments is just unbearable. You have seen that in the movies. Ooh, just so scary."

"I understand why you are afraid. Somehow, I don't think it would be like that for you," I tried to reassure her.

"See, that is the thing. No one knows what they would do because no one ever talks about what goes on in those places. So, it must be bad."

After we arrived, she became more subdued as we were sitting in the waiting room. She did not talk as much.

"By the way, do you want me to go in with you?" I asked.

"Yes, definitely."

We did not have to wait long before she was called back. As always, Marlene was recording the session to listen to later. Kara spoke in a very kind manner,

"Now, tell me what has been going on since your last visit?"

53

"I've been trying to cope with everything. My mind is still racing, lots of problems sleeping." She was talking rapidly.

Marlene started on one thing that soon led to another. She just continued to talk, on and on.

Kara had a hard time getting her to stop,

"O.K., now we will discuss that more in depth next time."

"Well, I need to tell you one more thing before I stop," Marlene said. As she was talking, she hesitated a minute.

"Whew, I am feeling dizzy. The chest pains are back."

"Marlene, do you have your Klonopin with you?"

"Yes, I think so."

"O.K., just break the tablet in half; put one half under your tongue, and swallow the other half.

"Whew ... www, these are deep pains ... it hurts to breathe."

"Just relax, and take some deep breaths. I am almost sure it is a panic attack," Kara spoke calmly.

"I can't believe I am having an attack right during the appointment."

"Try visualization. I am sure you have done that in the past."

"Do you mean visualize calm scenes?"

"Yes, do something that relaxes you, such as calm music. Some people enjoy going into their flower garden or playing the piano. One lady enjoyed housework, believe it or not. I had one guy who loved woodwork, but I told him that could be a little hazardous. Try something relaxing to divert your attention and calm you down."

Kara left the room for a few minutes, and then returned. She chatted on a little until Marlene seemed to feel better.

"One of the things that may be affecting you is your predisposition to noticing the differences. You seem to have a heightened awareness of the changes in your body."

"I probably do."

"Also, we may need to change the dosage of the Klonopin. How much are you taking now?"

"I am only taking it when the actual symptoms begin for a panic or anxiety attack. I have had five attacks this past week. I have written every panic attack down since I cannot remember very much."

"Now, another consideration is that you will need to return to your primary care physician. Let him know you have had a recent EKG. Get him to refer you to a cardiologist to check out your heart, especially considering you had rheumatic heart disease and a heart murmur when you were thirteen."

"O.K., I will."

"I would feel more comfortable once you see a good cardiologist. And, you need to see him very soon. Also, I think you can start taking your Klonopin regularly, like in the morning and at night. You can take it preventative, three times a day, if you want."

"Oh, I did not know that."

"If you know there is a particular time of day that you are going to have one. Already, you have had what is called a 'precursor' (a previous event and it indicates the approach of another). If you are feeling what is called an 'aura,' or the sensation that one (a panic attack) is coming on, you can go ahead and take a tablet."

"Like tightness?"

"Yes, tightness or any type of feeling of anxiety."

"You can take a half of a tablet or whole. Some people say a whole tablet makes them too sleepy or groggy."

"Another thing I want to ask you about is my sleeping problem. I have been taking a tablet of Ambien, but I would sleep two hours and wake up. So, I 'upped' the Ambien to one and one half tablets; I have been sleeping better."

"Well, you should not 'up' (take more of) the Ambien. One tablet (10 mg.) is the most you should take. What you need to do is take a whole tablet of Klonopin instead to help you sleep. By the way, always check with the doctor before you change the dosage of your medicines."

"O.K., I promise I will check with him next time."

"Ambien is what we call a 'natural sleep-enhancing drug.' It produces a natural kind of sleep, the REM (Rapid Eye Movement) sleep; the downside is that it only lasts for four hours and then it is gone."

"Maybe that is why I always wake up after several hours."

"Yes, that could be. O.K., we will discuss all of these medications with Doctor Simmons when he comes in."

"What about food I eat? Should I cut back on caffeine, or anything?"

"It might help to cut back on coffee which can produce anxiety or hyperactivity."

"Once I decided to cut everything out all at once, but that was not such a good idea. I felt pretty bad."

"No, we never advise anyone to cut out everything overnight. So many drastic changes at once are not good. People can really get stressed out when they do that. We'll just tackle one thing at the time. Right now we are just trying to tackle your racing thoughts, calming you down, and getting you in sync. Since you are still having the racing thoughts, we may need to increase the Depakote. But the difference in you is remarkable in a week, don't you think?" (Kara directed this question to my sister.)

"I did not see her last week. Of course, my sister told me the situation whenever I talked to her on the phone . . . so, yes, just based on what she said, she is better. I think Marlene notices a difference," Marilyn said.

"Yes, I am a lot better than I was," I responded. "A week ago, I was pitiful . . . it took me thirty-five minutes just to fill out the form out front."

Kara started explaining to my sister about my diagnosis, "What it looks like is that Marlene has 'bipolar affective disorder,' which used to be called manic depressive illness. She has been go-

56

ing extremely fast. She had been very depressed in September, and then she started switching from one phase to the other. The switch was so fast that she was still suffering with some of the grief she had and with the upset from the depressed state. With the switch to the faster mode of thinking, it was flip, flip, flip (she motioned with her hand from one side to the other) back and forth from one phase to another. What we have done is given her medicine called Depacote, which is a mood stabilization drug; it is a lot like Lithium . . . we used to give Lithium."

Marilyn spoke up, "Yes, Marlene mentioned Lithium the other day, and my first thought was a Lithium battery, like I use in my camera."

I then interjected, "O.K. give me the battery, but where do I put it in?" Everyone laughed.

Kara continued, "She has also had some history of sadness on and off in her life."

"Yes, there is no doubt about that," Marilyn agreed.

"There is some family history that would lean toward this being a good diagnosis (bipolar affective disorder) for Marlene. I sent home a lot of literature last week. So share that literature and read up on it."

"I have a social worker friend as well as my daughter who just graduated with a degree in social work . . . so I have been telling them about the situation. My daughter understands a lot about bipolar disorder and the situation," Marilyn explained.

"The tendencies have probably been there all along, but it has been controllable. She has been a high energy woman with short periods of depression. Then, the short depressive periods started taking over, and what happened was she could not maintain the high level of energy any more. She began to be depressed all the time. Does that make sense?" asked Kara.

"Yes," my sister agreed.

"Then, it starts getting very scattered . . . so that the thoughts

57

get scattered, and like I talked about with Marlene . . . it can become pre-psychotic."

"Pretty much where I was," I added.

"Yes, that is where you were."

"I was so scared . . . confused," I added.

"It sounds like twenty-four hours after you were here, you became pre-psychotic. You were on the brink of becoming psychotic. Rapid cycling—you were switching very quickly from depression into the mania. That is why Dr. Simmons went ahead and put you on the Depacote as soon as he could."

"When he called me at home that night, I noticed his urgency."

"Well, you were coming off the Serzone. Anytime you are coming off an antidepressant, sometimes you can have an increased exhibition of whatever the underlying problem is. An antidepressant like Serzone decreases anxiety. As the amount of medicine went down, your anxiety went up. Overall, you seem to be doing pretty well, right now."

"I think I am doing better," I related. "One question I have is 'what illness do I write on my health form to be reimbursed?'"

"Actually, there is a diagnostic code for it, but you can just write, 'mood disorder' to get reimbursed."

"Another problem for me is financial. My insurance will not cover your services as a clinical nurse specialist. So, I don't know what to do."

"We can find you another place to go if you want to."

"Actually, I want to continue to come here, but I may not be able to afford it. I do feel that you are helping me."

"I will discuss this insurance coverage with Dr. Simmons and see what we can do."

"Great, I appreciate it," I said.

"Also, we were talking about literature; there are some books for you to read, such as *Call Me Anna* (1987) by Patty Duke.[1] I have another book called *Mood Swings*,[2] I can't remember the au-

58

thor, but someone else has it now. Anyway, you need to be more stable when you read it . . . it might scare you."

"O.K., now I was wondering, 'What are your plans for me?' I know everyone is different and the medicine varies for everyone. How long does it normally take to treat someone in my condition, and how long before I can return to work?" I asked.

"Well, it depends on what type of obstacles come up. If something traumatic happened, then that would create an obstacle. Generally speaking, I tell people it is just like when you break a bone . . . you are going to give yourself four to six weeks for that bone to knit, right?" Kara asked.

"Right," I said.

"Then, you are not going to go out and run a race right away on that bone. You are going to give yourself physical therapy for about six months, at least, after that time period. So, that it makes the muscles build up stronger. Generally, after an initial problem like this, as severe as yours was, then four to six weeks minimum until you are going to feel like you are down to some baseline. Then, probably about six months after that until you are back completely feeling good and normal again."

"Right."

"And, usually what happens is, if people have a lot of history to deal with, a lot of problems, and it sounds like you have a significant amount of history. . . ."

"Yeah, I do."

"Then, you may want to stay in therapy . . . until you feel better," she related.

"Ummmm."

"People stay in therapy . . . well, forever . . . and that is fine. It is a good way to deal with the issues. I think it is great."

"Sounds good . . . you (i.e., one can) keep getting things out instead of holding them in," I added.

"You mentioned you tried to do some of that mental work before, but maybe it was not the right time. Or, perhaps, your mind was not in the right frame of reference to hear some of the things because it needed to have a balance. It was not balanced."

"I really think I have been in this, this, uh . . . *condition* for a long time."

"I think you have a true chemical imbalance; it is really biological. Plus, you have had a great deal of stressors in your life."

"Yes, I have. I really don't know when this chemical imbalance began."

"Well, you mentioned your first depression was back in high school. So, we know there was a predisposition (hereditary linked you to this disorder) back then, so this gives us a pretty good genetic link. You mentioned that your grandmother had a nervous breakdown, right?"

"Also, her sister had mental problems."

"It sounds like there was a biological predisposition for you," Kara surmised. "O.K., let us stop here, and I will find Dr. Simmons."

(Marilyn recalls.) After a lengthy conversation, Kara left to go update the doctor about the situation. All of a sudden, Marlene started crying and said, "Marilyn, I cannot go home."

"What is wrong?" I asked.

"I need to go into the mental hospital. Can you go tell them for me?"

I was taken aback since she had been adamant about her fear of a mental institution, and the horrors of being tied down and given shock treatments.

About that time, Kara returned to our room. I told her what Marlene had said. So, again, she conversed with Dr. Simmons. Soon he came back into the room,

"Marlene, are you sure you want to go into the hospital?"

"Well, I don't *want* to go, but I know I have to," she replied.

"What made you change your mind?"

"Something is wrong . . . my mind is out of control. I can't keep going like this. But, I am very afraid of the mental hospital."

"Don't worry, we will take good care of you."

"But, I do have some questions first. Would it be possible for you to treat me in the regular hospital?"

"Actually, no, you have to go through the entire program that is provided within the mental hospital."

"O.K., well, can you promise me that ya'll won't tie me down, or put any restraints across my mouth?"

"Oh, we don't use any kind of restraints. I can definitely promise you that."

"What about shock treatments?"

"No, nothing like that. We have a very caring staff to help you. Our whole purpose is to see you get better."

"I am ready then."

"O.K., who do you need to call at home?"

"My husband."

Marlene knew he was planning a trip out of town, but she did not seem particularly concerned or upset about it.

"I need to call your physician in Milledgeville to get some paperwork sent from his office. Do you have that number?"

"No, I don't have it," she replied. Then, she said, "Oh, yes, I do. The Milledgeville phone book is in my car."

Of course, it was in her car!! Everything else was in there—why not the phone book?

"I will go make preparations, and get the paperwork started to get you admitted right away," the doctor said.

A man of courage is also full of faith.

—Cicero

Eleven
The Mental Ward

(Marilyn continues.) They were able to admit Marlene at once. So, we drove across the parking lot where the mental facility was connected to the main hospital. By then, it was around 5:30 or 6:00 P.M. I knew Mother and Daddy would be expecting us soon.

We headed on in for her to be checked in. The usual paperwork, questions about name, address, etc. Then, the clerk stated, "You will have to clean out your pocketbook. Give your driver's license, money, anything valuable to your sister. You won't need them. Plus your watch, rings, all your jewelry."

As Marlene was going through her billfold, she said, "I don't guess they will want me to have this—my gun permit," she laughed as she handed it to me. In spite of everything, she knew what she was doing, and had not lost her sense of humor.

As I was leaving to unload the car, I jokingly inquired, "Do you have a bellhop to help us since she has so much stuff?" I asked rhetorically. "Obviously not." So, I went to the car and got EVERYTHING!

(Marlene.) The clerk continued collecting information. Then, she asked, "Are you suicidal?"

My heart was pounding . . . but I knew what I had to do.

"Yes," I robotically replied, thinking that "yes" was my key to admittance.

Although at that particular moment I was not feeling suicidal

63

at all. I remembered that another clerk had mentioned that I had to answer 'yes' in order to be admitted. I probably would have been admitted according to the doctor's orders, but I did not dare take that chance this time.

According to what I remember, someone had said, "No one can force you to enter a mental hospital; you have to admit yourself."

I was shaking . . . Here I was . . . about to enter a place that had always conjured up such scary thoughts and images. I had made so many mistakes in my life. I hoped this was not another one. God gave me the courage to admit myself . . . there was no other explanation.

In addition, she explained some rules about the hospital. We could wear our own clothes. We had certain visiting hours, in the evening; no visitors at all on Monday or Thursday nights. The one that stuck out in my mind was, "Your family cannot contact you for the first forty-eight hours." *What a strange rule*! I thought. But, I did not ask. At the time, signing papers and hearing rules seemed so minor to me compared with signing myself into a mental ward.

Had a brief assessment with Barbara who took my vital signs—blood pressure, temperature, etc. She was the friendly and helpful lady whom I had spoken with by phone a few weeks earlier.

Then, Karen came to escort us upstairs. The door for us to enter the mental hospital was locked; someone on the inside pushed a button, the lock clicked, and Karen pushed the door open for Marilyn and me to enter. Everything looked very clean . . . but plain, gray, and empty.

Or, maybe that was my state of mind.

We walked down a hallway and stopped at an elevator. I do recall vividly that a key was needed to unlock the elevator for us to get on. The thought of being locked in or out was scary. When we got off the elevator, I looked back as she locked the elevator behind us.

*My mind was in such an odd place that being locked in did
not upset me at the time. Under normal circumstances, I could not
stand being locked inside a place. When I was small, it seems I got
locked (or stuck) in a closet, and I never forgot it. I don't remember who or where it happened, but it was a traumatic experience. I
hated that feeling of confinement.*

After I got upstairs, my blood pressure was taken again. I
don't know why. Did they compare my pressure from downstairs
until I reached upstairs, a few minutes later?

Karen read me all the information about the smoking rules.
We could not smoke in our rooms, and no one could have their
own matches or lighters. We had one central smoking room located on our floor. Normally, I did not smoke on a regular basis,
just during stressful times. Of course, the past month, or so, I had
begun smoking at home again. So, I signed the form stating I
would abide by the rules.

The designated "Smoking Room" was fairly devoid of deco-
ration . . . chairs were scattered around, some placed around in a
semi-circle. I remembered there was a small TV. What stood out
the most was one large cigarette lighter toward the front of the
room . . . my first thought was this was an "industrial strength"
type because of its size and starkness. It reminded me of the small,
steel switch box used as an electrical outlet which is normally hidden within the wall. This lighter was equipped with a flip top and
was attached to the wall with a heavy, coiled wire. No one could
walk off with it . . . that was for sure.

Karen then walked me down to my room on the corner. As I
remember . . . the room was spacious, and plain with two twin
beds, a built-in desk space, linoleum floor, and a door leading to a
separate toilet and shower. She said,"Right now, you are alone.
You may get a roommate, at any time."

"Good, I had rather be alone."

Thank heavens!! No roommate, yet! Good, I could be alone

and to myself. With my luck I thought I would end up with a room-mate who was a screamer, or moaner.

Then, she took me on a tour of the floor. She introduced me to an older lady dressed in a skirt and crocheted sweater. In the beginning, I thought she was a volunteer and one of the staff. She started talking to me and walked with us to the small "patients only" refrigerator filled with fruit, crackers and drinks. She was the sweetest person and reminded me of someone's grandmother. I had no idea that she was a patient just like me.

(Marilyn's memory.) So, I dragged almost all of Marlene's worldly possessions up the elevator and down the hall to her room. The lady seemed amused about the conglomeration of things. I explained that she had planned to spend the week at our parents' house. She responded,

"Actually, she will only need her clothes. Very little else will be permitted here. We have to inventory every single thing she has."

So, Marlene and the lady started sorting through her baggage. I left them to go to make phone calls to our parents and family. I attempted to explain to my parents where we were and what we were doing. My parents did not really understand much about Marlene's "depression."

"What does she have to be depressed about?" they asked.

"According to the doctor, a lack of certain chemicals in her brain has brought on this behavior," I explained.

After several phone calls, I returned to find my sister and her helper still going through everything. I pitched in to help with the process.

"Marilyn, I guess I can't keep all of this stuff—it is going to be such a hassle to inventory everything. I am sorry you have to take all this stuff back down to the car."

Afterwards, Marlene and I walked down to the kitchen to get a snack . . . we both ate a banana. Then, I took everything back to

66

the car and filled it up once again and headed to my parents' house with her things. I knew upon dismissal that she would need to go there at least for a while.

(Marlene.) Meanwhile, Katrina told me the list of no-nos: we could not have straight pins, safety pins, toothpicks, nail clippers, scissors, a razor, razor blades, matches, lighter, a mirror, or anything sharp . . . any object that we could hurt ourselves with was forbidden.

We could have: Photographs with no glass in frame, flowers in plastic containers with no wires, plastic combs and brushes, stuffed animals, non-aerosol hair spray or mousse. Also, we could keep battery operated radios, travel alarms, and personal cassette players with a no-record feature on it. (It did not matter since I did not have any of those things.) I could keep shampoo, deodorant, and lotions, but only if they were in plastic containers. So, almost all of my toiletries had to go.

My sister was surprised during the inventory that I had cigarettes with me. She had never seen me smoke. Actually, I rarely smoked unless I became very stressed out. Probably, around six to seven cigarettes a day, at the most.

Later, I realized something else about the inventory. I knew they had to be absolutely sure we had nothing to hurt ourselves with. I had no intentions of harming myself now. Much later, the thought hit me . . . they were afraid we might hurt someone else, too. Of course, hurting another person was the farthest thing from my mind.

Katrina was very kind, and brought me my towels, wash cloths and toiletries that I could have. Then, she warmed up my supper of vegetable sticks, broccoli, turkey and dressing, English peas, roll, lemon cake, and tea. I ate well, and it tasted pretty good.

Then, Katrina left and returned with a urine specimen cup. At the time I considered it a normal hospital evaluation. Later, I wondered, *Was this a drug test?*

A few minutes later, Faye came in and did a lengthy assessment of my health status. Pages and pages of detailed information . . . medicines, all surgeries, family history of illnesses, on and on.

For anyone who has ever been in a hospital, you are familiar with the clerical routine. A continual stream of different individuals come into your room. Each one will ask a thousand questions, learn your life history, and write it down on a form. Then, a different person comes in and you repeat the same procedure again. You are thinking, "Hello, people, why don't you just Xerox my information and pass it on?" However, I was not really annoyed with this procedure, as I normally would have been. I felt they cared about my well-being.

After she finished that process, then, it became a little more interesting. . . .

She asked, "Can you tell me the last three presidents?"

I believe I knew them.

She said, "Now, I will say four words and I want you to repeat them, in order. Do you understand?"

"Yes."

"Pencil, blue, chair, heart."

I repeated them.

She said, "I will ask you to repeat them again in a few minutes."

A few minutes later, she asked, "Do you remember the four words I gave you?"

"Sure—pencil, blue, chair, heart."

I guess I passed the test . . . I don't know.

Everything here seemed plain and clinical. I was beginning to relax a little. Mostly exhausted but also relieved . . . just exhausted from the events of the day and relieved that the doctor said he could help me.

My preconceived notion about a mental hospital was that you had countless hours to sit around and do nothing. That was not true here. (Maybe, the philosophy was that being alone to dwell on our-selves was not a good idea.)

We had a daily schedule which everyone who entered the fa-cility had agreed to follow. Wake up call was at 6:30 A.M. with breakfast at 7:15 A.M. and medications at 8:00 A.M. Various morn-ing sessions with lunch at 11:45 A.M. and meds at 12:15. In the af-ternoon we had focus groups, activity therapy, group and individual therapy. Supper was at 5:00 P.M. with meds at 6:00 P.M. Our only alone time was a few hours after supper. Lights out at 11:30 P.M.

Our treatment program involved a high level of patient in-volvement. For our progress and recovery, it was essential to fully participate in the daily schedule. Even though we might not feel motivated, our attendance at all scheduled activities was manda-tory. All policies and rules were expected to be followed. I was agreeable with everything so it was not a problem for me. I just wanted to do whatever it took for me to get well.

Patients were expected to take all three meals in the hospital cafeteria. Any guests in the hospital were limited to coffee or juice from the kitchen on our floor. There were specific amounts of food and beverages ordered to cover only the needs of the patients. Our dress code was casual wear: jeans, slacks, sweatsuits, or walking shorts. No short shorts or halter tops. Sleep wear was not permitted in the halls or dining area.[1]

Several friends called that night. We did not have phones in our rooms. There was a phone down in one of the activity/lounge rooms. Someone would come get us if we had a call. We could not receive a phone call during any therapeutic actitvites. Calls could be made or received between 7:30 A.M. and 10:00 P.M. Later, I found out that no one could call me unless they had my patient identification number. Our privacy was protected that way so that no one could just call the hospital and find out who was a patient here. I believe my friends called my parents to find out the proce-dures of how to get in touch with me.

69

Of course, this being the year 1997, the cell phone rage had not hit. So, we did not all have portable phones like everyone does now. Not having a phone in my room was not upsetting to me, and I never questioned why we each could not have our own phone.

At 9:30 P.M. my medicine was brought to me in a little cup. The nurse watched me intently as I took it. Later on, I realized what was going on; she had to make sure that I took all of it. The staff had to be extremely cautious in case I did not take all of the pills; they never knew if one of us might try to hoard our medicine for a potential overdose. Most of us had probably expressed some suicidal tendencies at some point before we arrived here.

After that I headed down to the "Smoking Room," where around ten ladies or so, were smoking. I walked in and headed toward the lighter. One lady seemed to take great pride in operating the switch to release the flame. She lit my cigarette for me, and I found a chair near the front. Smoking was always my way to rebel. I felt comfortable being there.

Then, I decided to go and get my new tape of "Red Skelton." He was a comedian we watched on television as children. So, I headed back to my room, found it and brought it back to the smoking room. Watched it for maybe ten to fifteen minutes . . . not as funny as I remembered. No one else was interested; don't think anyone even glanced at the TV. Went to bed at 10:30 P.M.

Slept till 2:00 A.M. Woke up with slow, heavy ache in my chest; sat up and read for a while until I got sleepy again. The ache lasted most of the night—was one of those aggravating panic attacks. Should have called the nurse; don't know why I didn't.

Friday, Oct. 17

A young, black man in his thirties, maybe, woke me up at 6:30 A.M. to draw my blood. Afterwards, we all went into a small alcove together and waited our turn for him to take our vitals . . . temperature, blood pressure, etc. As we sat there, there was a little chit-chat. Not much. I did not really feel like talking much. The older ladies appeared sweet and seemed very calm and harmless.

I noticed last night that some of the ladies spent a lot of time in the Smoking Room. Whenever we had a brief break between sessions, certain ladies made a beeline for the room. The TV was always on, but no one ever watched it, at all. The main thing was to smoke and talk a little. I probably only went two to three times a day . . . smoking reduced some stress for me. Plus, my smoking helped me feel connected to the group; of all the different situations in my life, this was one time, I did not want to feel like an outsider.

I liked the hospital atmosphere so far. Everything was quiet here . . . low, low stress atmosphere. Although there was a schedule, there was not the feeling of rush here or rush there. Everything seemed low key. I was not afraid now. I felt safe with the patients as well as the hospital staff. All the attendants were kind and gentle. My doctor was nice-looking, thorough and attentive to my needs.

We were free to roam anywhere on our floor. I could leave my room anytime to visit the other TV room, snack or smoking room. The snack room was great; the cabinet was filled with crackers, snack bars, bananas, milk, etc. No food from outside of the hospital was allowed to be brought in. We could serve ourselves anytime. My appetite was not great, but I ate because I needed to stay healthy.

I noticed a locked glass door which separated us from another ward. I asked another patient in our group who was over there.

"Oh, that is the teenage ward."

"Why are they locked in a separate place?"

"Goodness, girl, some of them have been on drugs and could get violent, you know."

No, I did not know. But, the thought of it startled me a little. As a matter of fact, I did not know anything about this place. I had never known anyone who had been here. I had never even talked

71

with anyone who had entered a mental ward. All I knew was I was here to get help.

8:00 A.M. Time for us to go to breakfast. I started getting ready a few minutes before early so they would not have to wait on me. I heard the call and walked down the hall to the locked elevator. At first, the locked elevator had frightened me because I am claustrophobic. Slowly, it was becoming part of our daily routine, and I usually talked with the others as we went down to the cafeteria and made the return trip. I never experienced the twinge of fear or felt the walls closing in on me.

There was an attendant waiting for all of us to arrive. When everyone was there, he unlocked the elevator and took us down to the cafeteria where we all sat together to eat and talk. Part of the rules here—to be together for all activities. Several medical personnel stayed with us while we ate, but I don't remember who they were.

8:45–9:00 Medication.

We all returned to our rooms or to the smoking room after breakfast for a few minutes. Then, I heard the call for medication. I walked down the hall to take my place. Everyone was forming a line. An attendant unlocked the glass door which led to the teenage ward, but he did not let us go very far. We stopped at a small room where I saw a closed window. Everyone already knew, except me, to line up in front of that window while several ladies within the room prepared the medicine. So, there we stood all lined up like sheep to receive our meds (hospital lingo). For the most part, we stood there without saying much. I did exactly what the one before me did. I was the newest kid on the block so I had to learn the ropes. They checked each type and amount of medicine very carefully for us and asked our names.

I really tried my best to make sure I was taking the right medicine at the right times. I believed that the hospital staff was efficient, but I had previous experiences when the medical staff was not so efficient. At a doctor's office, a nurse had almost given me

72

another patient's shot. Luckily, I was assertive enough to question it before the mistake was made. Very scary . . . I had learned to be wary. When my turn came to get my medicine, she asked me my name, handed me a cup of water and a small cup of pills. She watched intently to be sure I swallowed all of them. Since I had entered the hospital, they had still kept me on Effexor for depression, Depacote for the mood swings, Klonopin for panic attacks, and Ambien for sleep.

My dosage for Depacote was 650 mg. which was a high dosage. The doctor was working to stabilize my mind which was racing out of control. His goal was to restore the chemical imbalance and get my mind on a normal level. Also, he wanted to control the ups and downs, going from depression to mania (control the mood swings).

No roommate so far. Only seems to be about six to seven of us here now on our particular floor. Today is Friday, and someone told me that yesterday they released six people, and a few the day before that.

Group Therapy

The leader gave us a handout and explained some of the rules regarding the group, and our hospital stay. All of the activities and services offered to us are to meet our needs and assist us in choosing options to solve the problems we have encountered. The activities are designed to help us in particular ways and they urge us to participate in everything that is offered. The experiences may range from dealing with very painful feelings to expressing humor and laughter. They offer us opportunities to grow, become stronger and hopefully enjoy happiness in our lives.

We were asked to keep names confidential within the group. Also, we should not discuss any information a person talks about or shares; we must realize what we hear is confidential informa-

73

tion. If we talk about it, especially outside of the hospital setting, it could be very damaging for that person. Patients were encouraged to be supportive, but not "give advice." Each patient needed to actively work on his issues and not get caught up in others' problems.

She reminded us to be respectful of each other's privacy and personal space. Opposite sex patients are requested not to enter each other's room. Intimate physical contact is prohibited. Patients are urged not to meet outside of the hospital while on therapeutic care. No loaning of money or engaging in business deals.[2]

Being involved with another patient never even entered my mind. I could not even imagine that. Apparently, that involvement had been a problem at times since there was a rule against it.

I liked the lady giving the instructions and conducting the session. After that, all I could remember was she told a story about fear which I found interesting. A few folks spoke up. I did not want to say anything; did not want anyone to know me or anything about me; it was pure drudgery thinking about myself; that was all I had done for weeks . . . sick and tired of my thoughts . . . wanted to get outside of my mind.

Then, it started . . . more chest pains, right during the session. I was embarrassed to stop the session, but I told them my symptoms. A few minutes later, a nurse came in,

"Here is your tablet of Klonopin."

"Thanks, ya'll are good to us here," I whispered.

She watched intently as I took the tablet and drank the water. (I don't know if I broke it in half and let it part of it melt under my tongue or not; I may have swallowed the whole pill.)

"Listen, anytime you need Klonopin, just ask for it."

"Oh, I was not aware that I could do that. I thought I could only take it at designated times."

Felt a little better after a while.

11:00–11:20 A.M.

On the way to AT (Activity Time), Dr. Simmons came down the hall to talk to several of us. I remembered thinking what a godsend he was. I was amazed at his memory. He knew the exact kinds and amounts of medicines each of us took, which ones he needed to change, etc. without looking at any notes or writing down anything. He added Klonopin as a regular med for me. He also said he was faxing the forms to take care of the "Sick Leave Pool" at work. I thanked him over and over for everything he had done for me.

We went down on the elevator to the small gym where there was a basketball court. I picked up a basketball and started shooting. I was the only one who actually engaged in any type of physical activity. I still felt lightheaded, but I really thought the exercise would do me good. The rest of the group headed on out the door to the small courtyard and sat at the picnic tables. I don't know what they were talking about or doing since I was inside the gym. Then, it began to rain so everyone headed back in and the attendant took us on the elevator back to our floor. We headed to our rooms.

Someone came down to tell me I had a phone call. My husband called to see about me. Also, he wanted to update me about the house situation. He was still dealing with a realtor about our buying a bigger house in an older, nicer neighborhood. The haggling back and forth on the price of the house upset me before I even entered the hospital. And, now, the house negotiations were the last thing I needed to think about. I don't remember anything else about the conversation.

A few minutes later, my mother called. My parents had certainly been great about seeing me through thick and thin. Then, my daughter, Ashley, age twenty-one at that time, called to see how I was doing. Both of them were so sweet and concerned about me.

We finished lunch around 12:15, and then was the call for meds. Like little sheep we followed, and lined up, waiting patiently. Even though I was not my "normal" self, I still saw the

75

scene to get our meds in a comical way. I joked and laughed with some of my "patient" friends about us being like little sheep following one another to get our medicine.

After that we had "Rest Time" until 1:10 P.M. At 1:15 we headed down to "Activity Time." They showed us to the Arts and Crafts area where we could work with wood, or paint glaze on different animals, and other items. I began working on a key rack since collecting old keys was a hobby of mine. I really enjoyed this activity, and it was a wonderful diversion for me.

Then, I laid down on a sofa in the Activity Room and rested. I was waiting to see if anyone else called me. Felt sad and empty. Here I was . . . a college graduate, former airline hostess, high school teacher and mother of two (plus two stepchildren) . . . a person with intelligence, now lying on a sofa in a mental institution. Very depressing.

Every now and then, the phone rang, and I walked down the hall to get the person. That was our system here. Soon, I fell asleep until we headed down for supper at 5:00 P.M. Very good conversation with the little group I am getting to know while we ate . . . four females and one male. Wish I had written down what we talked about.

6:00 P.M. Time to head for meds.

Then, someone mentioned that tonight was movie night, so some of us watched a movie from 7:00–9:00 P.M. in the Smoking Room, *The Mirror Has 2 Faces*[3]—don't remember anything about it at all. Then, I had to go check with the nurse; they had forgotten to give me Ambien for sleep. See, I told you; you have to be vigilant about meds.

Went to bed about 9:30 P.M. and slept well until they woke me up the next morning.

Saturday, Oct. 19

6:30 A.M. It seems to be my routine for the man to wake me up and take a vial of my blood. Plus my vitals—blood pressure and temperature. After he left, I started crying softly to myself. I missed being in my own bed at home with my husband. I was lonely. I wanted things to be the way they used to be . . . when I was well.

I got up and took my shower. My legs and underarms were beginning to get hairy, but they had taken my razor. I just could not worry about my appearance, other than staying clean.

Then, I began to pray concentrating on the following verse: Trust in the Lord with all thine heart and lean not unto thine own understanding. In all thy ways, acknowledge Him, and He shall direct thy paths. Proverbs 3:5–6.

I ate breakfast with three of my patient friends. I really like the older lady who was the first patient I met when I entered this place. She is very sweet. She is suffering from depression since her husband's death and is overwhelmed with some other family issues. Because of confidentiality, I cannot divulge her name, hometown or any other information about her.[4] But, she is an absolute dear. Another friend is closer to my age, and I am enjoying getting to know her. Unfortunately, I cannot remember anything about the third friend.

Some discomfort and chest pains today.

Got two phone calls . . . one from Mama and one from my son, Ty, who was fourteen, at the time. It must be difficult for them to understand what is going on. The main thing is: I know they love me, and I need that stability. But, there is nothing tangible they can do to help me right now. I need to be in this place.

After meds, they called me down to take a chest X-ray. The doctor had ordered these because he is concerned about my chest pains. He wanted to rule out any other medical issues, such as heart problems.

Group Therapy

Our whole group was required to go to these group sessions where we sat in chairs placed in a circle. I soon learned that their mission was to get us to open up and talk.

"Does anyone wish to share anything?" the leader asked.

No way, Jose . . . that was the last thing I wanted to do. My guard immediately went up. But, others start talking, little by little. So, each session was getting harder for me because the pressure was on.

"Marlene, why are you here?"

"It is hard to talk . . . about . . . it," I choked back the tears.

"Getting it out will help," she encouraged.

Finally, I gave in and "spilled my guts" . . . crying and telling the gist of my life story.

"Well, I have been through a lot. Pretty much overwhelmed with health issues, marriage, divorce, my son's surgeries . . . on and on. Lots of trauma and stress for years. Finally, I could not take it anymore and wanted to end it all."

It was such a personal thing to tell strangers my secrets, but somehow, I got it out. As I talked, several people in the group nodded their heads as if they understood what I was talking about. Maybe, they identified with my pain. After that, the sessions got a little easier.

As I was going to "Activity Time," Dr. Simmons along with his assistant stopped me. He had a lot of information to share with me. He wanted to let me know about my paperwork . . . my copy of the sick leave pool policy, which he had signed and faxed to my workplace. The policy was great for extended sick periods, such as mine. I could use sick leave from a "pool" where co-workers donated their extra sick leave hours.

One of the assurances here was that we saw our doctor *every* day.[5] I could not believe it; he made his rounds without fail. I was impressed. Unlike any other hospital I had ever seen.

Then, he assisted me with the "Request for Family/Medical Leave" to get it filled out correctly.

"Marlene, you remember my diagnosis for you was 'mood affective disorder,' or bipolar disorder."

"Oh, yes, I definitely remember. I was glad my illness had a name."

"O.K., well, let me caution you on something," he remarked in an agitated tone. "Your illness and its name is privileged information."

"Yes, sir."

"On these forms, the only words you should write beside 'illness' is 'mood disorder' . . . nothing else," he said emphatically. *I had not heard him speak in such a defiant tone.*

"I understand."

"Your diagnosis *is only your business, mine, the nurses, your family, but not your workplace.*"

Gosh, Who had set him off? Had my director at work needled him about my diagnosis? Whatever occurred, he was adamant about protecting my confidentiality. I was so surprised, and my mind was too cluttered at the time to even ask him what had happened.

"O.K., another concern of mine is your husband. What was his reaction to your coming to the mental hospital?"

"Well, normally, he does not say very much. So, I guess he was O.K. about my admittance. He went on a trip out of town."

"Normally, we like for the entire family to be involved with your wellness here and your return home. I just wanted to be sure he agreed with your being here."

"Yeah, I think so," I replied.

"But, we have plenty of time to discuss that later."

"O.K., I understand."

"As far as your panic attacks, I want to increase your dosage; start taking one half tablet of Klonopin morning, noon, and at supper. Then, take one full tablet at bedtime. Hopefully, this will lessen the chest pains. Also, I am cutting back on your Pyridium for your kidney problem. It seems to be much improved."

"Thank you, Doctor. I appreciate your help."

"Marlene, you are doing fine. Things are going to get better. Any other questions?"

"No, not that I can think of."

The attendant took me on down to Activity Time which was Arts and Crafts. My mind switched quickly from the previous conversation as I starting painting the second white coat of paint on my key rack. I became completely absorbed in the process.

After about ten minutes, I was called away while they attached a halter monitor to my heart. The plan was that I would wear the halter all the time. My instructions were: Press the button whenever I felt unusual pain. This occurrence was labeled as an "Event."

They let me return to Arts and Crafts for a little while longer. I painted the first white coat of glaze on my two ceramic bunny rabbits. I just realized something . . . everything I worked on I used the non-color, "white." Maybe white symbolized something about my condition.

About 11:20 A.M. I left the arts and crafts area, and headed back to my room. I needed to continue my journaling before I forgot the previous conversation with my doctor. Also, I had become very, very tired. I did not feel like talking any more or doing anything.

Also, I am a little worried about a patient friend of mine, Sally. She checked out today. She is probably about twenty years younger than I am. She just entered the hospital on Thursday with a breakdown of some sort . . . I don't know exactly. So, this was just her third day here. Her family did not seem to understand the seriousness of their daughter's situation. Or, maybe, they were like most families; they were embarrassed for their child to be in a mental institution. At any rate, they were very anxious for her to leave. This is just my opinion: BIG MISTAKE for her to leave so soon. Apparently, they had found her a job, or something. I don't think she will be able to handle it; she seemed unstable to me. Of course, this is coming from someone who is a patient myself. We are sworn to be confidential about others here so I cannot say anything more.

11:45 A.M. Mealtime.

Now, I am learning the schedule. I headed down the hall to the elevator. We stood around until everyone arrived. The attendant took us all down together to the cafeteria. I am getting used to his key locking and unlocking our passage to meals; maybe, it is for their safety as well as ours.

Individual Therapy

My time to go in with the counselor by myself. I took some notes from her talk with me:

1. Learn to love myself.
2. Make my life with my immediate family a "haven" for myself. Work on creating that safe place, and do not worry about anyone else. I have been taking care of everyone else in my family, but not myself.
3. She suggested a book for me to read: *A Brilliant Madness* by Patty Duke.[6]

My counselor seems to be kind and sympathic to my needs. She does not come on too strong. I think she really wants me to get well.

5:00 P.M.

Supper—Ate chicken strips, lima beans, hashbrowns, one half muffin and chocolate milk.

5:45 PM. Medication:

Depacote, 125 mg.—1 tablet (mood stabilizer)
Effexor, 37.5 mg.—1 tablet (depression)
Pyridium, 100 mg.—1 tablet (kidney problem)
Klonopin,—one half tablet (anti-seizure, panic attacks)

Stood in line, not impatient . . . just tired. After that, I dragged myself back to my room. I was very weary . . . maybe it was the medicine causing me to feel drained. I had cried three times that day . . . of course, crying has always zapped my energy.

Then, a Wonderful Surprise! My daughter, Ashley, walked in around 7:00 P.M. Visiting hours were 6:30–8:00 P.M. I was so tickled to see her! She brought me flowers, a little Snoopy Halloween bear (holding candy), Reeses candy (my favorite) and *Southern Living* magazine. (All flowers had to be in plastic containers.) We sat out in the Activity Room, and she met two of my best (patient) friends, and some of their family. We watched a little of the *Jeff Foxworthy* show. She was so sweet and stayed about an hour.

Then, my Mama called to talk and catch up. My son (fourteen, by now) had arrived at her house, and was very disappointed that I was not there. But, this was one time that I could not help it, and I did not have to feel badly about it. (According to my therapist.)[7] Ty said that he, Mom, and Pop would come to see me the next day.

Sunday, Oct. 19
7:00 A.M. The man woke me up to take a vial of blood. This time I teased with him, and said,
"Look, don't ya'll already have enough of my blood?"
He half-laughed, and said, "Well, I guess not."
I knew they had to keep testing my blood level due to the Depacote I was taking. It could cause liver damage.

Got on up and took a shower. Headed down to the elevator, but only a few people showed up to go to breakfast.

8:00 A.M. Meds.

9:00 A.M. Group therapy with the same lady as my individual counseling sessions. She was wonderful!

After that, a lady came by to remove my halter heart monitor; had it on from Saturday, 10:30 A.M. to Sunday, 10:30 A.M. Still having the dull chest pains on and off, but I guess they will let me know if the pains are heart-related.

10:00 A.M. Arts And Crafts

Almost finished my key rack; completed painting on two bunny rabbits . . . they are ready to be fired. Stayed longer until 11:25. There is another patient who enjoys this time as much as I do. She and I started talking and joking . . . I said I wonder if we could still come to the Arts and Craft time once we are released from the hospital. She said she would love to continue to come, too.

Dr. Simmons came by to see me. He seemed O.K. with my progress. He talked about my medicine, and asked about my panic attacks. He said he would let me know the outcome of the heart monitor.

I called Mama, and the line was busy. I then called my sister Dianne and gave her the information about what I wanted Mama, Daddy and Ty to bring to me.

Ate lunch, went for Meds, but did not go to Activity Time; I don't know what the activities were . . . too drained and sad to participate. I just took a nap on the sofa in the Activity Room where the phone was. Every now and then, the phone rang and I took messages for people.

Around 3:45 P.M. Mama, Daddy and Ty got here. Visiting hours for Sunday were 3:30–4:30 P.M. and 6:30–8:00 P.M. I was very glad to see them. They brought me some more clothes, stationery, mail and paperwork. They had checked out a book by Patty

83

Duke, *Call Me Anna,*[8] about manic depression issues and had brought it to me. They stayed about an hour.

At 6:45 P.M., my friends, Terry and Cathy, came to visit me. They brought roses, cards, and candy. Great to see them! Enjoyed their visit!

Then, that night my sister Dianne called, and also called my daughter Ash for me. My sister Marilyn called and then got in touch with my friend Janet. A little later, my friend Pam called as well as Janet; they are my true blue friends.

Have become accustomed to the routine . . . have become comfortable and no longer have fear of any harm being done to me. Our group seems to be non-violent, mostly depression, bipolar, and such, so far. The counselors had advised us about our safety. If another patient confides in us, such as, telling us secrets about someone being harmed, we must inform the staff. A secret involving our safety had to be reported.[9]

I am in the "place" where I should be right now. I have not been afraid when I go to bed at night even though we do not have locks on our doors. This place does not feel strange to me now. I feel safe. I know God is watching over me.

This particular mental hospital is not at all like I had imagined. I have not seen the use of padded cells, strait jackets, shock therapy, or anything like that. Maybe, other areas of the mental hospital have these things . . . I don't know. I don't remember ever asking anyone about it.

That night, felt more chest pains. Also, woke up during the night to go to bathroom; could not empty my bladder. Discomfort woke me up. Emptied bladder, a little more, walked around, emptied more.

Monday, October 20

5:00 A.M. Woke up, needed to go to bathroom again, more problems. A few hours later, they took a urine sample.

7:00 A.M. Nice man came as usual to take my blood. This time

I remarked, "Gosh, I gave yesterday; they must really like my blood."

"Yes, I guess they do," he sort of chuckled.

8:00 A.M. Breakfast with our group; three to four of us enjoy talking during meals now. I can't remember what we talked about now. My new friends here are very important to me; I feel connected.

Afterwards, off to Meds. Here we go, one after another, little sheep.

9:00 A.M. Great Group Therapy with Joe.

Took lots of notes. He talked about levels of "Enlightenment." As time goes by, we gain knowledge and insight by looking back and learning from our experiences. That is "enlightenment."

Part of the enlightenment is "unlearning." We go through an "Unlearning" process in that we will have to "unlearn" our old bad habits of thinking and acting. It may take 100 days to "unlearn" a thought pattern. It will take a lot of discipline to actually change one thought. Many things that helped me for years may not be helpful to me now.

"Progress, not perfection is the key. We can make progress, but our goal should not be perfection,"[10] Joe told us.

Example of wrong thinking: "When my job gets better, I won't be depressed." That is wrong thinking. The truth is: "If I am O.K., then my job will be O.K." I have to make the changes in myself.

One patient shared, "When my mother dies, or my son gets O.K., then I will be better. I will get better when they get better."

The counselor explained, "Well, actually, let us re-think that thought. Each of us has to 'fix' ourselves first in order to improve. We cannot wait for the situation to change for us to change."

Someone asked, "This is a different subject, but what do we call ourselves? I mean, what is the correct term now for people with mental problems?"

Several people spoke up. Someone said, "We are labeled as 'neurotics.' "

Someone else said, "Mostly we are called 'psychos.' "

Jokingly, I said, "How about 'loonies'?" No one laughed. We never resolved what the "politically correct" term for us was now.

Later, after that session, I called my friend Diane. Gave her my information . . . I am in Room 66 and my patient number is 0560. She told me she saw my son Ty on television . . . something about a high school basketball game. Also, she said her mother had just died this past Saturday.

11:45 A.M. Lunch. I have been trying to eat although I still do not have a great appetite. The food is pretty good.

Dr. Simmons stopped me in the hallway. He spoke in his usual kind manner,

"Marlene, how are you feeling?"

"I am feeling pretty good; maybe a little drained."

"Are your thoughts still racing?" he inquired.

"Actually, my mind has calmed down a lot."

"Good, that is what we are striving for. What about the panic or anxiety attacks?"

"Well, I am still having the pains slightly, but not as much."

"Your chest X-ray was clear and the results from the heart monitor showed no signs of a heart problem. That is good news. Hopefully, the Klonopin will control your panic attacks . . . they should lessen."

"Good, that is a relief."

"Marlene, you are doing well."

"Thank you, doctor, for your help." He walked down the hall as I headed to the med line.

12:15 Meds.

1:00 P.M. Group Therapy Session with Lynn.

She gave us a handout, on "Chronic Mental Illnesses." Most mental illnesses are caused by a chemical imbalance in the brain. They are treatable through medication and therapy designed to help cope with the stress and manage the illness. A major barrier to successful treatment of mental illness is non-acceptance by the patient, family and society.

My responsibility is: learn my diagnosis, signs and symptoms of my illness, understand my stressors, structure time better, take medication regularly and work with my doctor.[11]

She talked about "Regret and Guilt." Important difference. She talked about a particular situation when her daughter was born with a disease. She had mixed feelings of regret and guilt. She was filled with great sadness, and regret. Then, she began to feel guilty as if she had caused her daughter to get the disease. However, much later she realized great lessons had been learned through the situation. The regret was a healthy response, but the guilty part was not. Feeling guilty was entirely her fault.

(Notes I took from the hospital session.)

Plan of Recovery:

1. Plan what I will do when I get out (of the hospital). I am in treatment here, but my recovery is out there.

2. Pray the "Serenity Prayer." God grant me the serenity to accept the things I cannot change; the courage to change the things I can; and the wisdom to know the difference.

3. Patterns. The patterns of taking care of myself must change when I get home. I need to maintain a healthy lifestyle to meet my own needs. Then, I can be a better mother and wife.

4. Complete change. If there is any physical or sexual abuse in my life, I would have to get help right away. Does not pertain to me.

5. Growth is gradual, and takes time. Keep this in mind.[12]

5:00 P.M. Supper and meds afterwards.

No panic attacks today, except, just a slight little pain. Good, maybe the medicine is helping me.

No visitors are allowed today (Mondays) in the Adult Unit.

Tuesday, Oct. 21

6:45 A.M. Usual routine . . . Man woke me up and drew vial of blood.

"Good morning, didn't you get enough blood yesterday?" I joked.

"No, ma'am, I guess not," he replied.

"One of these mornings I may run dry, you know."

"Uh, huh . . . that is right," he sort of laughed.

Then, he tooks my vitals.

Continued with my routine: Took my shower, and went with group for breakfast. Then, to the med line, of course. *March, march, march, two, three, four, march, march, I still laugh to myself about our little rituals of getting our medicine, and lining up in our queue:*

Things always exactly the same. . . . State name, type of medicine, take small paper cup of pills, swallow pills with little cup of water, eyes watch me carefully, return empty cups to nurse, thank her, I turn to leave, and walk down the hall . . . same routine every day.

I now understand how a patient becomes so routine oriented and robot-like . . . day after day, year after year. Same routine . . . mind becomes so accustomed to the schedule that he may become agitated with any slight change.

8:45 A.M. Medication Class

A pharmacist came to talk to us about our medicine; I was very anxious to understand more about the medicines that I was taking.

Someone asked, "Can you tell us a little about Klonopin?"

"Sure, it is used for anti-anxiety and anti-seizure purposes. Normally, it starts with a low dosage. The nurse may take your vital signs frequently to make sure the dosage is right for you. Also, you can build up a tolerance for it so it may take a higher and higher dosage to produce the same effect. Often, used to treat panic and anxiety attacks."

He talked about antidepressants such as Paxal, Zoloff and Effexor. They affect moods, feelings and are slow working. Most may take two to three weeks to take effect. I told him I had switched from Effexor to Serzone.

"Do you think my changing my antidepressants caused my mania?"[13]

"Mania can be activated by several things, but usually not by a change in medication."

I was relieved that I was not directly instrumental in causing my depression to switch to mania.

Someone asked, "What causes mood disorders?"

He said, "A combination of stress and trauma. A child may experience early trauma, such as abuse, loss of a parent, or live in an alcoholic home. Then, a period of prolonged stress prevails until a stressful way of life becomes normal. At some point, a chemical imbalance occurs in the brain, and the person cannot control his moods. A mood disorder develops."

"What should the person do?" someone inquired.

"That is a good question to ask. First of all, get a good physical checkup, which may include a check of the pituitary gland and a brain scan. A mood disorder has good recovery rate so begin your mental health program with a competent psychiatrist. Be prepared for lifestyle changes."

"What about bipolar disorder?" I asked.

"O.K., the old term for bipolar was manic depressant. It is a combination of depression and mania . . . lows and highs. The trick is to maintain a balance between the two. The disorder is manageable with medication, good health habits, family support, therapy, etc.[14] Good session for me and some others. No panic attacks so far.

11:45 P.M.

89

On my walk down the hallway for lunch I saw Dr. Simmons and his assistant coming. I am always glad to see him.

"Good morning," he said. "Marlene, how are you doing?"

"Much better."

"Have your panic attacks continued?"

"No, just a little pain."

"I am glad. I believe the Klonopin has helped as well as the therapy here," he explained. "Also, I wanted you to know all of your paperwork concerning your sick leave at work seems to be in order . . . finally. We have tried to accommodate all the information your workplace wanted."

"Thank you. I know it has been a hassle."

"Well, I know you have been extremely upset about your work situation and the paperwork, but you can put those worries behind you now," he related. "Of course, we are much more interested in your health issues."

"Thank you. I am doing pretty well."

1:30 P.M. Group Therapy Sessions

The topic was about our support groups and things to help with our recovery. (From my notes:)

Phone calls which are reciprocal are a good support tool. By talking with our family and friends we give an inventory of our day, and they do the same for us. Good therapy.

A (patient) friend of mine said soothing tapes were helpful to her, such as sounds of the ocean, or rain, or quiet music. Another friend said the music from her mother's funeral was uplifting to her. (Funeral music seemed sort of depressing to me.) Someone else mentioned "visualization tapes." My understanding of these tapes is that you listen to the sounds of a rain forest or waterfall and concentrate on visualizing the calm, restful scene instead of problem.

Advantages for being an in-patient here: The staff can assess and observe our behavior by our actions. For example, if they notice we don't bathe, eat, or sleep, they will notify our doctor. These indicators alert him to the fact that we may be sinking into a deeper depression. Or, if they observe drastic mood swings, they report our behavior, and he will help us regain a balance through medication and talk therapy. It is not safe for us to be an outpatient if our symptoms are out of control.[15]

Arts and Crafts

Still enjoying this time a lot. Talked with girl, we always laugh about wanting to come back to the hospital during the arts and crafts period, even after we are dismissed. Finished with the ceramic rabbits so the lady said she would "fire" them today.

My daughter and good friend called this afternoon. I know my daughter loves me no matter what.

6:45 P.M. My good friend Diane from Macon came tonight during visitation hours. Glad to see her . . . she always makes me laugh.

9:15 P.M. Went to bed early. Slept well.

Wednesday, Oct. 22

7:00 A.M.

No one came to take a vial of blood. I don't know why, but was glad.

9:30 A.M. Session on Spiritual Issues.

The guy giving the session used to work here at this hospital. Now, Bill is a counselor locally.

He posed the following questions: What is it I value the most, or connect with the most? Do I value a belief in God? Do I only value others to the extent I am just a people pleaser? Do I depend on another substitute such as drugs or alcohol?

For our "Spiritual Recovery:"

1. Admit that I am not in control of the world.
2. Believe that God can restore my sanity (a quiet mind.)
   Bible verse: In quietness and confidence is my strength.

3. Turn over my will and my cares to God.
4. Surrender the control. Realize I am not in control of my husband, or my children. I am not in charge of them. I am in charge of myself and need to do what I am supposed to do to take care of myself. I only have to do this for a minute, then an hour, then two hours . . . just for Today. Do not try to be a martyr.
5. How can I achieve peace of mind? Through meditation, prayer, a clean heart and honesty, just for a start.
6. When someone wants me to do something, is that something that would be the BEST thing for me? I do not have do it because someone is telling me to do it. However, a different way could be what IS the Best Way for me. I will do something because I CHOOSE to do it.
7. What is wrong when I say that I am right all the time? It could be that something is too devastating, too painful, too embarrassing, too shaming, or too threatening. Maybe, I do not have a clear picture of who I am as a child of God. I have no sense of value as a human being. I feel worthless, or inadequate.
8. Whenever people put us down, they probably don't feel good about themselves. Bullying, meanness and prejudice are examples. If I feel O.K., I am happy with myself. I don't have to look down on someone else.
9. I must give myself the things that I am desperately seeking from someone else.[16]

One lady spoke up. She worked as a nurse and counselor full-time. Recently, her mother had died, and she was devastated. She took care of everything—the house, her husband, and children. She was just overwhelmed, and she felt her family did not help her or respect her as a person. Her eighteen-year-old son was now in a boot camp, and she had a child at home. The counselor suggested that she learn to be more assertive, and learn to say, "No." Also, be less of a people pleaser, and treat herself better.

"This discussion has brought up a good point. Now, I am speaking to everyone—many of us get into the 'people pleasing' business. If things are very unbalanced, we need to rethink and re-focus ourselves. The healthier thinking is: *I* must do what is best for *me*," Bill shared. (Later, he told me the same thing about being a people pleaser.)

A younger girl shared her story.

"I was raised in a small town where I was a telemarketer for a while and then, a waitress. Right now my boyfriend is on cocaine; I'm addicted to painkillers. I am in such a state . . . a state of confusion . . . I don't know what to do. I lost my father whom I really loved. My mother was always very cold, unforgiving. I have been married six times."

Of all the things she said, I was shocked to think she had been married six times and was younger than I was. I could not imagine. I had been married twice, and divorced once, and just those events were almost more than I could handle.

11:00 A.M. Group Therapy

The leader handed out cards with a word on it. Then, each person had to talk about what was on the card. My card had "Mother" written on it. I said my mother was a caretaker who attended to everyone's needs. She was a very good homemaker, constantly cleaning, cooking and washing all the time. Made sure we had everything we needed. Had a lot of friends, and visited the shut-ins. Was a constant worrier and highly anxious.

A few days earlier I shared some things about myself and my family. Talked about depression and bipolar issues. I imagine I had calmed down a great deal since I entered the hospital almost a week ago.

A new girl entered the hospital today and joined the group. She started rattling on and on without taking a breath.

"I have moved around a lot since my family was military; you can guess that I was an army brat. All of them are crazy, you know. My entire family has some sort of mental illness, so I have it, too. My husband and children come down to my shop all the time, and they are literally driving me crazy."

"What kind of shop do you work in?" asked the leader.

"Look at my hair; you can't tell that I am a hairdresser?" she snapped. Apparently, she loved being the center of attention. And, actually, she was an attractive person. She hardly paused for a response and took off on another tirade. She seemed highly agitated, nervous, and talked ninety miles an hour.

"Now, my customers are complaining; they say I never shut up; I am driving them crazy; but I can't help it."

All of sudden, she turned toward me. In a very aggravating tone, she snarled,

"You make me sick sitting there so calm like that."

I was so surprised when she said something directed to me that I don't know if I mumbled back a response, or not.

"I just can't believe you are bipolar like me."

I was not prepared for her sudden verbal attack on me. One thing I do remember about her conversation . . . her whole demeanor totally grated on my nerves.

Later, I wondered. Was this how I was acting before my treatment began?

11:45 A.M. Lunch and Meds.

No panic symptoms or attacks today.

Dr. Simmons came by my room.

"Marlene, do you feel you are making progress?"

"Definitely, I have learned a lot and I feel better," I answered.

"By the way, we did not take a blood sample today because the levels in your system seem to be fine."

"One thing I wanted to mention . . . something that surprised me. Another patient was upset with me because I was acting calm; she did not see how I could be bipolar."

94

"Well, I guess you will encounter that reaction at times not only here, but once you leave," he responded. "What did you say?"

"Actually, I was so surprised, I don't know if I said anything, or not," I said. "But, I am O.K."

"Great, we think you are doing well."

2:30 P.M. Activity Time.

I am still enjoying working on different projects in Arts and Crafts. I began working on a small "cricket stool" today. Guess what color I am going to paint it! White, of course.

7:00 P.M.

During visiting hours, my friends Terry and Cathy came. They are one of the most supportive couples I have ever known. Whenever I need them, they are there to help me . . . they are amazing.

Thursday, Oct. 23

Same morning routine; no blood drawn.

8:00 A.M.

A pharmacist came to talk to us about "Medications in Recovery." He told us, "If you are not sure about what medication to take, Ask! Ask! Ask! It is our responsibility." Also, he advised us to know the brand and generic names of our medications, know the dosage, and when to take them. Know what each drug treats, and its side effects.

"Can you explain about the drug Depacote?" I asked.

"Sure, Depacote is used today instead of Lithium because it has various dosage amounts which can be easily adjusted according to what the patients need. It works to stabilize moods. In the hospital we take blood often to check and interpret the effects of Depacote."

Then, he gave us a handout and talked about alcoholism and a cross addiction of drugs and alcohol.[17] I took some vague notes, but the information did not really apply to me. Not very interested.

9:30 A.M.Second session on Recovery.
Question: What will help us in our Recovery

1. Encouragement from family and friends
2. Positive attitude about managing disease or disorder
3. Look at my issues, but do not blame myself for illness
4. Openness toward solutions
5. When a family member or friend says, "Get a grip," or "cheer up," remember he is in denial about my disorder or does not understand
6. Counseling and therapy
7. Take a good look at my lifestyle—modify my destructive behavior patterns and try not to be so critical of myself
8. Be honest; if we hold secrets within, we will remain sick[18]

Video on Stress Overload

Understand that everyone has stress and strain in his life from work, children, parents, or many other things. Many things can add to stress, such as procrastination, perfectionism, being a workaholic, poor planning, no relaxation time, and on and on. Many times we don't allow enough time to do a certain thing so we are constantly in a hurry. We are under pressure to do more and more.

We should pace ourselves and give ourselves permission to cut back. Stop for a moment, take a deep breath, and relax when under constant pressure. Affirm that we have a right to feel good and healthy. Walk outside, or into a different environment for a minute.[19]

11:45 A.M.

Got on the elevator as usual to head downstairs to lunch. Our group is now comfortable talking with each other which makes things easier on everyone. We know our routine: get off the elevator, go through the cafeteria line, choose our food items to put on our tray and head to one of three tables assigned for us.

After we had eaten and chatted, we returned to the elevator for our attendant to take us back upstairs. But, today a new girl, probably in her twenties, got on the elevator with us. It was hard to ignore her—she was nervous, jumpy, and extremely talkative.

"Listen, ya'll, I really don't need to be here," she stated defiantly to everyone.

Silence.

"Really, I don't need to be here," she stated emphatically.

"Maybe you can just stay a few days," someone offered.

"You don't understand . . . I am fine . . . all I need to do is pray to Jesus, and I will be much better. I have got to get out of here." She seemed agitated and ready to climb the walls.

Someone whispered to me, "I think she's a drug addict."

"Well, you need to be here for a while," the attendant said.

"No, I can't, I can't. I don't even know why I am here. If I can go home, get my Bible, and pray to Jesus, everything will be O.K.," she repeated.

This encounter was unnerving to me . . . her demeanor, her attitude was so unsettling. At that moment on the elevator, I knew . . . I knew I was well enough to go home. My health seemed so far removed from her situation. I was on my road to recovery.

On the other hand, this young woman's journey had just begun. She was in denial of her situation, and I felt she was her own worst enemy. How could they help her?

Went to Meds.

2:30 P.M. Group Therapy Session

How to keep myself out of here (the hospital):

1. Take good care of myself—eat healthy, get plenty of rest, exercise, take time for myself, and socialize with friends.

2. My personal awareness of signs of hypomania and depression: too many racing thoughts, incredible ideas, poor thinking—judgment goes out the window, actions indicating intense anger or agitation, confusion, euphoric feelings and suicidal thoughts.

3. Educate family and friends on signs and symptoms of my disorder. They may notice a certain behavior before I do so they can make me aware of it. They can help me when I need it. It is interesting that even when family and friends learn to recognize the mood swings as possible bipolar disorder, the person may deny that anything is wrong.

4. Signs for family and friends: More irritable, intense anger, sleeplessness for days, eating too much or too little, hyperactive, excessive spending, altered states of up and down moods and talking about suicide.

5. Know myself well enough to go ahead and call the doctor when things change, and I know I need help.

6. Be in tune with myself: If painful memories keep coming to the forefront, I need to stop and pay attention. Healing comes with sharing so I should talk them over with my therapist.

7. Make changes at home that are necessary for my well-being. Ex: Have a calming routine for bedtime.[20]

Dr. Simmons popped his head into my room.

"Hey, how are ya?"

"Hello, Dr. Simmons, I am doing pretty well. When do you think I will be ready to go home?"

"That is strictly up to you, just depends on how you feel."

"I feel like I am ready."

"Let's see. You have been in here for one week. Do you think your family can adjust to any necessary changes for you?" he asked.

"Well, I sure hope so."

"You will need their full support to recover and maintain

your balance. Also, you can continue seeing me for your medication and therapy, if you choose. Or, I can recommend another doctor."

"No, I will definitely continue seeing you; you understand where I started and where I am now," I responded.

"Do you think I can be released tomorrow?"

"If you feel you are ready, I will start your paperwork."

"Yes, I am not 100 percent well yet, but I am ready to leave the hospital."

"Marlene, you have done very well so far. You need to try to relax when you get home; don't try to catch up on everything at once. Your mind and body have gone through some traumatic events, and you do not need to get yourself stressed out."

"Yes, I understand what you are saying. Do you think I can go back to work soon?"

"Not, yet. We will schedule you an appointment back in the office probably for Monday. You need more time to get yourself stabilized before you return to work."

"Dr. Simmons, I appreciate all your help. I promise I will continue to take my medicine and take care of myself. You don't have to worry . . . I will follow your advice."

Thursday night . . . No Visitation in Adult Unit.

Twelve

The Release

Friday, October 24

Today I am being released and heading home. I have mixed feelings . . . I am ready to go home, but a little afraid at the same time. I hope I can handle things once I get home and back to work. I do not want to have a relapse.

Don't remember many details about my departure from the hospital or the trip home. I did feel a little odd when I arrived to the house. When I opened the door, and walked into our den, I suddenly stopped. The den . . . this was the place where I had spent a lot of hours pacing up and down, pulling my hair, and moaning. But, things were different now . . . my mind was not racing, and that type of behavior seemed foreign to me.

No memory of my first weekend at home. Did not write anything down.

Monday, October 27

Returned visit to see Kara and Dr. Simmons.

"Marlene, how are you doing?" asked Kara.

"Much better. Being on the medicine for a while has helped. The hospital experience was good; I learned a lot about my disorder, the medicine, and ways to cope with what I have."

"You now understand that your disorder was genetical—so you realize that it is just part of your chemical makeup. You had no choice in the matter."

"Right."

"Also, you are very intelligent, which can become a definite problem for a person who is bipolar. You want to get all these things done, but are hampered by your disorder. Many intelligent people cannot accept this fact and they end up committing suicide."

"I know what to do now before I feel that depressed."

"Also, you have experienced a tremendous amount of trauma and stress in your life. While you were in the hospital there was a lower stress atmosphere, but returning to the outside world, you need time to adapt to the outside stress again."

We talked for a while longer.

"You have come a long way, but you are still talking fast."

"Am I? I did not realize it."

"I believe your mind is processing faster than it should. We most likely will increase your Depacote to slow you down a little more."

"Something we want you to start is keeping a daily mood chart. We will give you the forms so you can write exactly how you are doing each day. Hopefully, we will see a pattern to your ups and downs; thus, we can make adjustments to help keep you balanced."

"That sounds fine to me. What does Dr. Simmons think about my return to work?"

"Let's ask him."

When Dr. Simmons walked in, I almost wanted to cry. Without him I don't know what would have happened to me.

"Marlene, you are doing well. I want to increase your Depacote just a little, and give your body time to adjust to it. We will continue to monitor it."

"Thank you so much, for everything. When do you think I can go back to work?"

"Well, your body has been through a lot. You need a little

more adjustment time so you can most likely return in one week. Remember to take things slower than normal."

"When should I return here?"

"For a while we will see you every week. Then, we will progress to two weeks depending on how you are doing."

"Thank you again."

November 3

I returned to work at the library. At first, I was somewhat apprehensive, but I was determined to prove I could make a comeback, mentally and physically. I did not talk very much about my hospital experience during this time to anyone. It was all too fresh and too painful. And, I really did not concern myself with what people thought about my visit to a mental hospital. I kept my mind focused on catching up on my work and taking care of myself.

In the beginning, fatigue was my biggest problem. Many times, I ate a little lunch and took a brief nap to survive the afternoon. Little by little my strength and energy returned.

So, what is my present situation? It has been ten years since I was in the mental hospital. One year after my release, I transferred from the library to a recruiting job in the Admissions department (at the same college in Milledgeville). I was ready for a change. The new position was great since traveling and public relations were a better fit for my personality. I traveled for four years, and now I am working back in the Admissions office.

As far as my health, many people are surprised when they realize I am bipolar. I talk openly about my disorder and share any insights when people inquire. I am no longer ashamed of my illness. In fact, many people seek me out to talk about depression, panic attacks or bipolar issues.

Writing this book has been extremely beneficial for me. I have gained a great deal of insight and understanding about my mental problems as well as others. And, yet there is always more to learn, such as this past weekend when I returned to my hometown.

Sunday morning we decided to drive to McDonough (Henry County) to visit my parents. I started asking my dad more about our family history concerning any mental problems.

"Daddy, when did your mother have a nervous breakdown?" I asked.

"Right after my daddy died; they had been together for so long . . . it was very hard on her and she just could not take it."

"I vaguely remember something about that. Now, they would probably diagnose her with depression, or something similar," I said.

"Maybe so."

"Also, she was depressed after several children were born," my mother added.

"Did she get better?" I asked.

"Yes, after a while she was O.K."

"Did anyone else have mental problems?" I asked.

"The only one I knew about was her sister Essie."

"What happened to her?"

"Well, she and Uncle Willy got married even though they were on up in age . . . late fifties, I believe. He built her a new house. When they moved in, her demeanor started to change."

"Gosh, I wonder what upset her."

"Well, they did not know. Except, you see, she had lived in the same house her entire life," my mother interjected. " Many of the tasks she had done were unnecessary in their new home."

"Maybe that change was too much," I said.

"Anyway, the neighbors said that after Uncle Willy and Aunt Essie moved in, they could hear her . . . almost every night . . . hollering and hollering . . . most of the night.

"What ever happened to her?"

"Well, finally, there was nothing else Uncle Willy could do to help her; so, he admitted her to Central State Hospital (mental hospital) in Milledgeville for treatment. The physicians did whatever they could to help her.

"I never knew anything about that."

"Little was known about treating the mentally ill back then. I don't know how long she was there—six or seven years or so, and eventually she died."

I did not remember hearing my family talk about this situation before now, and I was surprised to hear about it.

As I was finishing up this book, I decided to drive on the other side of town for lunch . . . to a small café where the best Southern homestyle baked chicken, vegetables, sweet tea, biscuits and desserts are served. I got my usual tray to go.

As I left the café, I found myself taking a right turn instead of a left. I began heading away from the university. I don't know why; it was almost as if something or someone was drawing me that way. A spur of the moment decision. A few minutes later, through the trees I spied a gold dome on one of the prominent buildings at Central State Hospital. I had not driven by there in many years, and it was a gloomy sight. I turned down the driveway and passed many dilapidated buildings with rusted screen across the partial porches, broken windows, and sagging curtains. In 1847 this hospital complex (State Lunatic Asylum) once housed many of the "pauper" mentally retarded and insane patients within the state of Georgia. At one time its population rose to around 12,000 patients—actually too many for the staff to take care of. So, some of the conditions became deplorable compared to standards today. It had greatly downsized in recent years so many buildings were empty.

As I rode past the old buildings, my mind started to put the pieces together. Now, I began to understand my initial sadness when I read the article about the old cemetery out here; it was a strange premonition to my connection. My dad had given me the clue, and my mind started processing . . . what he had told me.

Now, I even knew *who* had drawn me to this place as well as why. It must have been Aunt Essie—she was my connection. She had lived and died in one of these buildings, in 1966, but she did not get the chance to tell her story . . . what she experienced, how she felt, what she thought, . . . that may forever remain a mystery.

But, "why" did she want *me* to come here? Possibly to open my eyes to the realization of many things: I was fortunate to live in modern times with excellent mental hospitals, medications, and trained psychiatrists! Fortunate . . . to recuperate with the help of counseling, group therapy, and medications. Fortunate . . . to regain the mental capacity to write down my experiences, and truly blessed to return to live an almost normal life.

Maybe the reason "why" I was drawn to this hospital was to emphasize the necessity for me to write about my personal experiences with mental illness and maybe some day to write about the tragic past of my great Aunt Essie and many others.

I know I cannot change what has passed, but I *can* share my story and become an advocate for all people suffering with mental health disorders.

Thirteen

Explanations and Clarifications

The second part of the book will explain and clarify details concerning the contents. Naturally, I cannot explain every detail about depression, mood disorders, bipolar disorder or psychiatric hospitals. Therefore, I have only hit the high points of my limited knowledge since an entire volume could be written on each one. All of these mental disturbances are complex, and affect each individual in different ways. I am posing questions and answers which I believe will be most beneficial.

One point I definitely need to clarify was the situation about my sick leave and work. It was a misunderstanding on my part and the administation. My thinking was confused, and I thought I was doing what I was supposed to do. I may easily have misunderstood my role in taking care of my sick leave . . . I am not sure. I did have my local physician send the director a detailed letter concerning my illness at the beginning of October.

During my absence from work I still do not know what procedures the administration took, and now it is a moot point. But, several co-workers told me different things about what was going on, which truly bothered me. Someone said they were upset because I was getting paid for not working. Eventually, all of the details got taken care of, which was a huge relief to me.

Also, regarding the comments my supervisor wrote on my yearly performance evaluation, he was most likely correct. On several evaluations, he wrote about my "incongruent" behavior and the "quirk in my personality." At the time, I was furious at him for writing these comments. It is interesting now because I realize how blinded I was to my actual behavior; at that time, I did not see any truth in his words. I thought something was wrong with him.

Even with all the symptoms known by physicians, it is not always easy to diagnose any of these illnesses. If a person shares most of his symptoms and circumstances, a more accurate diagnosis can be made. Naturally, many times we do not want to share everything about ourselves, especially if it is embarrassing or personal. Therefore, due to the lack of details, many people have been misdiagnosed, given the wrong advice, and wrong medicine. When their situation worsens, they do not return to the doctor, which can be a tragic mistake.

I feel it is important for everyone to be educated on the signs and symptoms of mental illness. Some of the symptoms may overlap, and some may be connected with a totally different problem. If you think that a friend or loved one is experiencing some of these difficulties on the following pages, please encourage them to seek professional help. But no one can force them into treatment;it is a personal and voluntary decision.

How Can You Tell the Difference Between Being Sad and Being Clinically Depressed?

Sadness is a temporary brief period of feeling a little sad or blue. It may last from a few days to a week, and usually the person feels better.

Clinical depression is persistent and interferes significantly with an individual's ability to function. As a serious medical condition, depression affects mind, mood, body, and behavior. Everyday habits may drastically change, such as a person may stop bathing, washing his hair, and brushing his teeth. His appetite may drastically increase or decrease, and he may sleep too much or too little. Even making a very simple decision becomes difficult. Also, overwhelming feelings of helplessness and guilt may be prevalent which is different than the ordinary "blues."[1]

Clinical depression is an imbalance in the normal chemical processes of the brain which a person cannot control. It is one of the most common and treatable mental illnesses. Studies indicate about nineteen million adults suffer from this disease, in the United States.

The American Psychiatric Association has identified these symptoms as potential signs that a person is suffering from depression. If a person experiences four or more symptoms for more than two weeks, professional help should be sought.

1. Noticeable change of appetite
2. Noticeable change of sleeping patterns
3. Loss of interest or pleasure in activities formerly enjoyed
4. Loss of energy, feelings of fatigue
5. Feelings of worthlessness or complete hopelessness
6. Feelings of inappropriate guilt, feel that everything is my fault
7. Inability to concentrate or make decisions
8. Recurring thoughts of suicide
9. Overwhelming and prolonged feelings of sadness or grief
10. Recurring and prolonged unexplained headaches or stomach aches[2]

A depressive episode is diagnosed if five or more of these symptoms last most of the day nearly every day for a period of two weeks or longer.[3]

What Causes Depression?

Depression can be caused by many things: lacks of self-esteem, inherited traits (genetics), suppressed emotions, anger, loss of loved one, or loss of job. There are so many variables and combinations that it is impossible to list them all. A licensed psychiatrist or therapist can evaluate and diagnose someone with depression.

When there is a family history of depression, a person may have the inherited traits or be biologically inclined toward the disorder. Evidence shows that the amount of chemicals in the brain can change and be a significant factor in causing depression. In addition, persons with certain characteristics—pessimistic thinking, low self-esteem, a sense of having little control over their lives, negative thinking patterns, and a tendency to worry excessively are more likely to develop depression. Significant losses, financial problems, or major change in life combined with excessive stress can cause an onset of depression.[4]

With clinical depression a person cannot control his depressed state. A person cannot mentally "will" himself to "feel better" or "cheer up." To expect someone to do that is like asking a person with cancer just to stop having cancer.

Also, this type of depression may not necessarily be dependent on external circumstances. A wealthy person who has the finest home, job, great children, and highest level of education can experience depression as easily as someone who has very little.

Someone can start out being sad and grieving about something. If it continues, he may become unhappy, miserable, and bitter until the depression becomes a part of his personality. Many symptoms may become apparent, such as he may stop bathing, or washing his hair. Loss of interest in everything. He may reach the phase where he cannot function. A major depression is when he has suicidal or homicidal thoughts, and he can't trust himself.[5]

While researching information for this book, I discovered

why only bad memories took precedence during my depressive episodes. Painful, childhood memories were emerging on my first trip to the doctor with my sister. There is a description of melancholic depression that almost perfectly described how I felt. "A preoccupation with minutiae and past failure steals away normal concentration, driving out any sense of joy. The skills to adapt to changing circumstance are lost. In their place exist painfully diminished energy and negative self-perception. Life becomes a burden, and for some, with deepening social withdrawal, a numbing preference for death emerges, born from the dark hopelessness that seeps into every facet of life.[6]

Another statement that verified why remembrances of the "bad" emerged instead of the "good" was also described "the sadder the mood, the more morbid are the memories that the depressed person recalls."[7]

When I began to have more and more depressive moods, I was not aware of family members having experienced depression. When I went through my ordeal, then more information came to light bit by bit about my relatives. Mental issues were still kept a secret.

Can Someone Be Depressed and Show No Visible Signs or Symptoms?

Yes, depending on the person. I was able to hide my depression for many years. And, as strange as it sounds, I was not aware that I was suppressing anything; I was merely coping with life. Mainly, my depressive episodes only lasted a few weeks, and then I returned to normal so no one really noticed. I stayed at home and did not discuss the situation with anyone. So, my friends were shocked to find out about my problems with depression because I was always upbeat when I talked or was with them.

Through the years I sought counseling and took several types

110

of antidepressants on and off. Being a resilient person, I pushed myself through the depressive phases, and usually things got better. Also, I continued to pray and relied on my faith.

For a long time there were no visible symptoms to the outside world of my depression until I reached that critical point . . . the point of no return, when I could no longer hide my emotions. Like a cracked egg, all of the contents came pouring out; there was no stopping it. No way to put it back and no way to uncrack the shell. The ugly outpouring was a conglomeration of pent-up emotions, and smouldering unresolved issues and inconsistencies.

Treatment for Depression

1. Appointment with licensed psychiatrist or therapist
2. Medications
3. Continual professional counseling
4. Education of family members

What Is a Mood Disorder?

A mood disorder is a treatable medical condition involving extreme changes in mood, thought, energy and behavior. It is an actual physical illness involving a chemical imbalance that affects the brain. Also, studies now show that there are actual changes in the structure and functions of the brain. The exact cause is not known, but it is not a character flaw or sign of weakness.[8]

A mood disorder may begin early in life, or it may not appear until later on. As in my case, my "mood affective disorder" did not appear until I was forty-seven years old. Many studies conclude that it can be genetic in origin, which means it typically runs in families. Trauma during childhood, such as incest, molestation, alcoholism, losing a parent early, or many other causes may contribute to developing a mood disorder.[9]

In addition, a person may experience a significant prolonged period of stress, day in and day out. "Stressors" or "triggers" are whatever causes a person to become extremely stressed out. A combination of stressors may initiate a mood disorder. These stressors cause the symptoms to get worse, and are different for each person.[10]

Then, at some point, the combination of triggers, trauma and stress can create a chemical imbalance in the brain, which is manifested as a mood disorder.

What is Bipolar Disorder?

Bipolar disorder is a type of mood disorder and is the modern term for manic depression. It is a brain disorder that causes unusual shifts in a person's mood, energy and ability to function. Different from the normal ups and downs that everyone goes through, the symptoms of bipolar disorder are severe. They can result in damaged relationships, poor job or school performance and even suicide.[11]

Bipolar disorder causes dramatic mood swings—from overly "high" and/or irritable to sad and hopeless, and then back again. The down is depression and the up is mania. There may be periods of normal mood in between. Severe changes in energy and behavior go along with the changes in mood. The periods of highs and lows are called "episodes" of mania and depression.[12]

Signs and Symptoms of Mania:

1. Increased energy, activity and restlessness
2. Excessively "high," overly good, euphoric mood

3. Extreme irritability
4. Racing thoughts and talking very fast, jumping from one idea to another
5. Distractibility, can't concentrate well
6. Little sleep needed
7. Unrealistic beliefs in one's abilities and powers
8. Poor judgment
9. Spending sprees
10. A lasting period of behavior that is different from usual
11. Increased sexual drive
12. Abuse of drugs, particularly cocaine, alcohol, and sleeping medications
13. Provocative, intrusive or aggressive behavior
14. Denial that anything is wrong[13]

A manic episode is diagnosed if an elevated mood occurs with three or more of the other symptoms most of the day, nearly every day, for one week or longer. If the mood is irritable, four additional symptoms must be present.[14]

One symptom which was evident to others was extreme irritability. It began while I was still at work, but I was not aware of it. Then, it manifested itself when I was demanding to see the doctor about my kidney infection. At the time I thought something was wrong with the receptionist; that she was not compassionate. I did not realize my demeanor was overbearing.

Toward the beginning of this book, I mentioned a strange sensation of feeling lightheaded and dizzy; almost as if my eyes and brain were set back an inch away from my skull, and I was preoccupied with my swirling thoughts. Did not feel like myself but almost as if I was watching myself (see p. 4). Of course, I never described this experience with anyone. Another person described a similar sensation as "a sense of distance and being an observer" which became a familiar experience to him, and who during mania felt himself a passive pawn in a larger purpose.[15]

Hypomania

A mild to moderate level of mania is called hypomania. Hypomania may feel good to the person who experiences it and may even be associated with good functioning and enhanced productivity.[16]

For several days I enjoyed the boundless energy and productivity of "mild" mania, which I have since heard that people like to experience. Unfortunately, my mind did not remain at that level. I was "rapid cycling" (shifting to the next phase quickly).[17] I had absolutely no control. My mind was buzzing constantly with the incessant "noise" of my racing thoughts. My thinking became more and more confused. My body was getting more and more tired, but I could not sleep or slow down to rest.

Without proper treatment, hypomania can become severe mania in some people or can switch into depression. Sometimes, severe episodes of mania or depression include symptoms of psychosis. Common symptoms are hallucinations (hearing, seeing, or sensing the presence of things not actually there) and delusions (false, strongly held beliefs and influenced by logical reasoning or explained by a person's usual cultural concepts).[18]

Mixed Bipolar State

Bipolar is an "affective disorder" that combines the polar opposites of depression and mania. A mixed bipolar state is when the symptoms of mania and depression may occur together such as a combination of confused thinking, agitation, increased physical activity and excitement.[19]

Treatment for Mood or Bipolar Disorder

If you know of a friend or family member displaying several symptoms previously described, it is necessary to get him to a licensed, competent psychiatrist who has treated depression, mood disorder and bipolar disorder. Be vigilant and check to see that the doctor gathers all the information before he makes a diagnosis.

Each psychiatrist may have his unique method of treatment, but most will treat it with a combination of medications, involvement of family members, regular scheduled visits, and "talk" therapy.[20]

If I Am Bipolar, and Start Feeling Better, Can I Stop Taking My Medicine?

Definitely not. The purpose of the medication is to maintain the balance of a person's moods. Antidepressants work to prevent a downswing in mood. The mood stabilizer, such as Depacote, prevents the upswing and slows the body down. It maintains the racing thoughts, excessive energy, etc.

The therapist works closely with the patient to stabilize his mood. It takes time as well as trial and error to find the right medicine and appropriate dosage for each individual. It can be a delicate balancing act.

If the person stops taking his meds, the chemicals go out of his system, and his symptoms will return. The longer he goes without the medicine, the worse his symptoms may become. Then, he has to start the process over again. It will create a setback because an antidepressant takes several weeks to take effect again.

The problem is that some people are opposed to taking medicine of any kind on a regular basis. They just do not want to be dependent on anything. So, once they start feeling better, they decide to stop taking their medicine.

Also, people do not like the side effects of the medications. Mood stabilizers, such as Depacote and lithium, slow down the energy level, metabolic rate, and generally cause a weight gain. Also, they may stifle creativity and productivity. Since people in (the mild or moderate) manic phase usually have lots of energy and can get a lot accomplished, they are resistant to taking any kind of medication that will slow down their productivity and creative minds.

More on Medications and Treatment

Toward the beginning of the book I mentioned my legs twitching at night. It turned out that it was a reaction to one of my medicines. The constant leg movement was not caused by depression itself.

When I first left the hospital, I made two visits to see my psychiatrist the following week. He was keeping close tabs on my progress. After that I saw him once a week. After the first year of my diagnosis, my routine became once every three months. That amount of time has worked well for me. Of course, whenever a problem has come up during the interim period, I have called him. His office is very accommodating about getting me in soon to see him, and I have been very satisfied with this arrangement.

One thing I want people to understand is that even though I am on medication at all times, I still go through depressive or hypomania stages throughout the year. It is the nature of the disorder—a constant juggling act. That is the reason anyone suffering with depression, a mood disorder or bipolar disorder must stay under a psychiatrist's continual supervision. I stay in tune to what my body is saying daily to keep myself stabilized.

When I first began taking Depacote and Effexor, it took over a year to get the right balance so that I did not feel too "up" or too "down." My psychiatrist continually counseled me, and inquired

116

first about any changes in my life, such as my job, health, children, or any new stressors. Then, he adjusted my medication according to how I was doing and feeling. If he increased the dosage of the antidepressant, then at times he decreased the mood stabilizer depending on my symptoms. Next, came a waiting period of several days for me to notice if I felt any difference—i.e., better or worse. At that point, I called him for another slight change in dosage, if necessary. He always advises me to call in 2–3 days if there is no improvement.

Even today the process is still the same; he adjusts my medications continually throughout the year. It is still a delicate and constant balancing act. Another factor that enters into this process is my honesty. I have to tell him exactly how I am feeling; at times, I still have the tendency to mask my feelings and not address them. I tend to think I can still handle everything myself when medication could take care of it for me. My belief is that without medication managing bipolar disorder is almost impossible.

My thoughts on antidepressants. After my hospitalization, and as my visits to my psychiatrist became routine, I expressed my thoughts about antidepressants. I told my doctor, there should be a quicker way than waiting two weeks for an antidepressant to take effect. If someone is truly depressed, he will commit suicide by then. My understanding is that shock therapy may be used, which acts more quickly. Fortunately, these treatments are much better than the treatments used years ago.

Why Was I Predisposed to Be Bipolar?

"Predisposed" meant that the disorder was hereditary. There was a genetic link for me (or other family members) to experience a mental illness. My grandmother as well as my aunts on my father's side have experienced depression and mental problems. Also, one of my sisters, and now my adult daughter have suffered

117

with depression. It seem apparent that genetics has definitely played a role, in our family's susceptibility to mental health problems.

Also, my personality has most likely increased my vulnerability to a mood disorder, i.e., my excessive need for approval which is often referred to as low self-esteem or low self-acceptance. A person with this trait depends on others for a sense of self-worth. Also, low self-esteem creates a fear of rejection that results in heightened sensitivity to criticism and difficulty in saying "no" to the demands of others.[21]

As the years went by, I suffered through continual trauma of various life experiences: divorce, health problems, serious surgeries, and a miscarriage. With the constant stress of working full-time, financial worries, and raising four children in a blended family, my mind became overloaded.

Therefore, it was a combination of many factors: genetics, my particular personality, trauma, and stress overload. Someone even mentioned the cortisone injections for my fibromyalgia could have triggered my mood disorder.

How Did You Know You Were Bipolar? How Did You Act?

Someone at work had asked me (June, 2006).

Actually, I did not know *what* was wrong with me. I thought I was going crazy. First I became very depressed, and then the panic attacks started along with the hypomania—high energy, rapid speech, inability to sleep, loss of concentration, confused thoughts, etc. It was a horrible experience being out of control and not knowing what was wrong with me.

What Are My "Patterns of Wellness?"

"Patterns of wellness" is a term I invented for managing my bipolar disorder. One key strategy in dealing with my disorder has been the simple word, *acceptance.* During my eight days in the mental ward, I:

- Accepted the fact that I have a lifelong disorder
- Accepted that I have to take medicine every day of my life
- Accepted my new lifestyle with a determination to manage it

I was anxious to do whatever it took to get better. I followed my doctor's instructions about everything. Most of my life I have led a healthy and fairly balanced life . . . eaten a balanced diet, exercised, prayed, relaxed, slept, and socialized. But, while I was in the mental hospital (October 1997), I became acutely aware of how important a healthy lifestyle is in managing my disorder. I realized how sleep deprivation for many years had taken a huge toll on my health. So, now I make sure that resting and sleeping are priorities.

Getting out and socializing with friends has always helped me tremendously. I am definitely a people person. Of course, at times, I still may withdraw if I start to go down; I still do not enjoy being around people if I am depressed.

I realize my medicine is as essential as my continual therapy. If I forget to take it, I attempt to catch up as soon as possible. I have my daily pill containers marked with each day of the week with the blue container for the morning, and the yellow one for bedtime.

I am still under the same doctor (psychiatrist) who treated me from the beginning, through my hospital confinement until today, almost ten years later. He not only understands my entire history, but we have an excellent rapport. That connection or rapport between the patient and physician is almost essential for success.

Also, as a psychiatrist he can monitor and prescribe medicine and conduct the "talk" therapy, or counseling.

My Christian faith and strong beliefs learned from my childhood have been a stabilizing force for me. In addition, during the 1980's I adopted "positive thinking" skills from Norman Vincent Peale whose works are based on Bible verses. The positive mental attitude has been a tremendous boost to my health; and my spiritual well-being has remained constant due to my dedicated prayer life.[22]

In addition, I have learned to avoid negative situations: sad movies, negative people, funerals . . . anything that brings me down. I know how vulnerable I am; and, how extremely sensitive I am to the impact negativity can have on my disposition, at times.

Exercise has always been an integral part of my life. I played sports earlier in life, and walking has been my constant exercise since then. I am aware of how important exercise is to my total health.

Several years ago my psychiatrist and I realized I had a pattern of sadness usually beginning in September each year. I began to feel depressed in the fall (just as the sap goes down in trees). He diagnosed me with SAD, seasonal affective disorder. Actually it is caused by the change and intensity of daylight, during the fall of the year. He adjusted my medicine accordingly, and I learned that sunlight is an important therapy for me. Thus, I have added sunlight to my wellness plan. I try to get outside every day for at least 15–20 minutes and sit in the sun. Even when it is cold, I wear a coat, and sit in the sun. For the past few years I have noticed that it has been helpful.

Then, I read about light therapy. Dr. Simmons mentioned he had other patients who had tried it with apparent success. So, almost a year ago I bought a (balanced spectrum) light therapy lamp, especially designed for people suffering with depression. It was fairly expensive ($175), but it has been very beneficial, especially through the fall and winter months. Dr. Simmons explained that it was beneficial only if I used it during the morning hours for two hours straight. In order to accomplish this, I set it over my computer desk at work. My depressive episodes have been milder since I began the light therapy so I feel the lamp has been helpful.

Since my diagnosis, I have never stopped taking my medications. One day, I remember saying to Dr. Simmons, "Please don't let me ever go into the mania phase again." He promised he would do his best to keep me stabilized. Fortunately, I have been able to stay on an even keel most of the time. I have not experienced a "manic episode" since 1997.

Does a Person with Bipolar Disorder Ever Get Well?

Managing bipolar disorder never ends. A person with bipolar must be on guard and strive to maintain a healthy lifestyle. There is no cure for bipolar disorder.

After all these years of dealing with bipolar disorder, I am still learning how to manage the illness. Recently (May, 2006), I became extremely agitated at work, and I could not stay on task. No concentration. I kept going from one task to another, but I could never get started on anything. I tried to get things done, but became overly irritable. I kept the feelings of irritability inside all afternoon and remained at work. I did not tell anyone.

The next morning I got up and started going through my routine to get ready for work. I was almost ready, and then I realized I should not go. The intense irritation was still there. I knew that I would end up arguing or yelling at someone. I was so agitated that I wanted to jump out of my skin.

Even though I have been dealing with the issues for ten years now, I did not know what to do to get out of this "funk." Other times when I felt a little agitated, I kept going until it passed. This time my body was telling me to stop.

So, I told my new husband (of two years) I had to stay home

because I did not feel well. I did not try to explain how I felt, then. I did not have the energy to explain the details involved. Although I did not feel sleepy at all, I slept on and off almost all day. At lunch, my husband brought a lunch of chicken and vegetables from town. I ate about half of it and went back to sleep.

I kept thinking, *If I sleep all day, I will be up all night.* By evening, my disposition improved . . . I felt calmer. It was very strange, but wonderful. Surprisingly, that night I was able to sleep through the night.

Actually, the plan of action I should have taken was to call my therapist. He has always told me to call him when I have problems. Many times I still try to handle them myself before calling him.

About a week later when I had my regular appointment with him, I explained my problem with agitation and irritability. He immediately understood the situation, and said my problem could quickly alienate my family, friends and co-workers. By increasing my Depacote (mood stabilizer) I should be able to tell a difference in a few days. Sure enough, I was amazed at the difference the increased dosage made. My irritation subsided and I felt good again.

Sanity, Insanity, and Suicide

Through my experiences with depression, panic attacks and bipolar disorder, I have learned one thing. There is an extremely *thin line* between sanity and insanity. I now understand how someone can go over the edge so quickly. The rapid cycling of depression to mania can occur very quickly. One minute a person is in great despair and a few minutes later, he has high energy, and is ready to conquer the world. He cannot think clearly, and everything can get out of control. If he is in the wrong place for treatment, then he could be easily misdiagnosed. If he is diagnosed as insane, proving otherwise could be difficult.

I have also learned that you never know what is going on in someone's mind. I appeared normal on the exterior, but my mind and thoughts were abnormal. A person may hide his depression or any other disorder like I did for a long time.

Interesting detail about suicide. Although several times during my life and particularly during the depressive phase in fall of 1997, I felt suicidal. At that time, no one was really aware of how helpless and hopeless I felt. Later, when I mentioned it to my family, they were surprised. Naturally, they did not understand my mental agony and there was no way that they possibly could.

However, I never thought about a certain method of suicide. That is, I did not actually stop and dwell on how I would commit the final act. My sister was the one who remembered that I had a loaded gun in the nightstand drawer although she never mentioned it to me, of course. I had not even thought about it. As it turned out, my loaded gun was in the drawer, the night I called the Crisis line for help.

My main message is that if anyone mentions suicide, take him seriously. Apparently, he is in a desperate situation, and the word "suicide" is his signal for help.

Thoughts on Stigma of Mental Illness

When I finally acquiesced and entered the mental hospital, I only did it because my mind was out of control, and I had reached the point where I could no longer fight it alone. The type of professional help I needed was the total program which was offered only within the confines of a mental institution. Naturally my reluctance was due to fear and my ingrained beliefs about mental illnesses and facilities.

In addition, in 1997 there was the tremendous stigma associated with mental problems so things were kept secretive. Until I was diagnosed with bipolar disorder that year, my family had mentioned very little about mental illness being in our family background. Slowly, I discovered that several relatives had suffered various mental problems in the past. But, no one had much to say about it. That was the normal way our American society dealt with mental illness, so, I am not being critical of their actions.

It has been interesting as I have written and talked about my experiences with mental illness. During a conversation, I might say, "Most people don't want to talk about a family member with mental illness." The other person will say, "Oh, everyone is much more open about that now."

That is when I think . . . Yeah, right. They are much more open until it happens to someone in their family. Then, it is still hush, hush. Everyone is still embarrassed about mental disorders when it hits home.

Recently, a friend and I were talking on the phone.

"Has anyone told you about Lynne's husband?" she asked me.

"No, what is wrong?" I asked.

"Well, we don't know; no one will say."

"Most likely it is mental," I said.

"His sister just said he was not able to be at work right now," she related.

"If it had been a physical problem, she would have said what it was."

"I guess so."

"It is frustrating that there is still such a stigma associated with disorders of the mind. And, I admit, it is not an easy thing to accept. We are all still worried about being labeled 'crazy' or being 'mental.' We know that once someone pins the label on us, we are stuck with it. Also, it may prevent us from getting another job if psychiatric help is on our record."

More Details about My Hospital Stay

While writing this book, I realized something about a situation that occurred during my hospital stay. It was concerning the hospital rules of "no family contact for the first forty-eight hours." My belief was that our two days was a necessary timetable for us to become comfortable and acclimate ourselves to the hospital atmosphere. I assumed the adjustment period made us more relaxed and conducive to the help offered there.

I realized the situation with the patient, Sally, whose parents took action on the third day probably led to the rule about no family contact for the first forty-eight hours. When that window of opportunity opened on the third day, her parents worked swiftly to convince her to leave and to check her out of the hospital. I felt strongly that she was not mentally ready to leave. Now, I understood the hospital policy about no family contact in the beginning, and I experienced firsthand how family interference could impede the progress of a patient.

Also, I wanted to further explain my thoughts about the girl on the elevator who wanted to leave the hospital, get her Bible and pray to Jesus. It is not that I do not believe that Jesus can change things. I definitely do. However, I also believe that He works through many resources—doctors, therapists, medications, and counseling. It seemed that everyone on the elevator that day realized she needed further help. And, I still wonder whatever happened to her.

When I entered the hospital the attendant told me there were certain things I could not keep in the hospital. One of the things was a razor, because I might harm myself or someone else. At some point, we were given a rules list about all our items, and I suppose I read it. However, I did not realize until I re-read the list recently that I could have asked an attendant to let me use a razor for a few minutes under supervision.

Also, I know there have been various changes in hospital policies since 1997. Since that time many companies and businesses have banned smoking within most buildings. So, I do not know if the patients still have a smoking room. Also, with everyone having a cell phone now, I don't know what restrictions there are on phone usage now.

What Is a Panic Attack?

According to the American Psychiatric Association a panic or anxiety attack is an unprovoked surge of fear accompanied by at least four of the following physical and emotional symptoms: heart palpitations, tightening in the chest, or shortness of breath, choking sensations, dizziness, faintness, sweating, trembling, shaking, and/or tingling in the hands and feet. Psychological reactions that accompany these bodily changes include feelings of unreality, an intense desire to run away, and fears of going crazy, dying, or doing something uncontrollable.

Panic attacks occur "out of the blue" when there is no actual danger—typically in familiar settings or situations. It may last from a few minutes to an hour.[23]

No one knows exactly what causes panic attacks. Periods of prolonged stress or a significant loss can instigate an attack. Holding in anger or sadness without any release. Or a chemical imbalance in the brain may be the trigger, but it is not a sign of mental weakness or personal failure.[24]

Coping with Panic Attacks

Klonopin (anti-convulsant, anti-seizure drug) was the first medicine prescribed to help me with these attacks. It is the same one I still use. Also, I have continued to use a very small amount, 5 mg. to help with sleep.

126

I have not had a full-fledged panic attack in many years, with the deep chest pains, shortness of breath, dizziness, etc. If I feel the sensation of a heart flutter, I put one half tablet of Klonopin under my tongue and let it dissolve. If possible I get away for a few minutes by myself and think of a relaxing scene or place, such as lying on a beach. I take deep breaths, and try not to dwell on my physical symptoms. Then, I resume whatever activity I am doing. After a few minutes, I usually feel O.K.

Over time you can diminish the intensity and frequency of panic attacks if you are willing to make some changes in your lifestyle. They include: regular practice of deep relaxation, regular program of exercise, elimination of stimulants especially caffeine, sugar and nicotine, learning to express your feelings of anger and sadness, and adoption of "self-talk" and "core beliefs" which promote a calmer and more accepting attitude toward life.[25]

Why Did I Not Write This Book Sooner?

For the longest time, I was not able to listen to the tapes or read my journal notes without getting upset. Every few years after my hospitalization, I attempted to read my notes or listen to the tapes, but almost immediately I started crying. The memories were too painful. I had to wait to get much healthier before I could handle writing this book. It has now been almost ten years, which includes the two years it has taken to write the book.

When I finally started listening to the tapes again, I was glad I had recorded myself. When I was talking, I constantly lost my train of thought. The harder I attempted to recall my thoughts, the worse it got. Plus, I spoke very rapidly and incessantly. I went on and on. I cannot imagine how my family and friends stood it. It was very aggravating to hear myself, and I must have sounded very much like the girl in the hospital who irritated me.

Even so, at times I had a hard time writing particular parts of the book. As I described certain events, I started to relive the moments and was overcome with pain and sadness. And, when I thought about my family, my children and friends having to go through this situation with me, it was disconcerting.

On the other hand, this past year when my sisters came down to visit us in the country, we were able to view it in a lighter way. We stayed up talking late into the night recalling the details about my illness, and we laughed about my obsessions—carrying the box packed full of information with everything in perfect order, and lugging the huge stack of clothes to my doctor's visit. I am healthy enough to look back now and see the humor.

Also, I will admit it has taken courage and conviction to take a stand and confess to the world I have a mental illness. Considering the fact I was raised in the society where speaking about mental problems was mostly taboo. In addition, I felt it was important to talk with my family about the impact on them as far as my openness. They have been supportive and encouraging toward my work on this project.

Another consideration was the possibility of relapse. After writing a book, what will I say if I have a relapse? What if I end up back in the hospital? Now, I know what I will say: I managed my disorder as well as I could, but I still needed additional help. I finally realized asking for help was not a sign of weakness, but courage.

Endnotes

Chapter Two

1. *Union Recorder* Newspaper. "Uncovering the Central State Hospital Cemetery" (September 1997). Article about overgrown cemetery and lost grave markers at CSH (mental hospital in Milledgeville, GA): Author.

Chapter Four

1. Symptoms about depression I read in a book in 1997, but the title and author are unknown.

Chapter Five

1. *Fifty Plus* magazine, supplement to *Union Recorder* newspaper, ("Those Were The Days," September 1997). My daughter brought me copies of this magazine.
2. Actual letter sent from my doctor to my library director on Wednesday, October 1, 1997; changed names of people.

Chapter Ten

1. Duke, P. and Turan, K. (1987). *Call Me Anna. The Autobiography of Patty Duke.* New York: Bantam Books. Account of actress's life dealing with manic depression.
2. *Mood Swings,* author unknown. Book mentioned by my clinical nurse specialist, which she wanted me to read at a later time.

Chapter Eleven

1. Psychiatric Hospital. Patient Rights, p. 3. Pamphlet given to all patients within the hospital.
2. Ibid., pp. 1–4.
3. Cayettes, Andre and Oury, Gerad. *The Mirror Has 2 Faces, (1996). Stars Barbra Stresiand and Jeff Bridges. Movie about two people changing to please each other.*
4. Psychiatric hospital. Patients' rights (1997): p. 3.
5. Adult Services Treatment Program, Psychiatric Hospital, *Patient Concern Resolution Guide* (1996): pp.1–3. Given to all patients in hospital.
6. Duke, P. and Hochman, G. *A Brilliant Madness: Living with Manic Depressive Illness.* New York: Bantam Books, Inc. (1992).
7. Individual therapy at the Psychiatric Hospital, October 1997. Counseling as well as literature on taking good care of myself first.
8. Duke, P. and Turan, K. *Call Me Anna* (1987). My parents brought me this book since they could not locate *A Brilliant Madness*, by Patty Duke.
9. Adult Services Treatment Program, Psychiatric Hospital. *Patient Concern Resolution Guide,* 1996: pp. 1–3.
10. Dyer, W. *Real Magic, Creating Miracles in Everyday Life.* (1992) New York: HarperCollins Publishing.
11. Robinson, R.A. "Chronic Mental Illness," *Patient Education Manual.* 1997: pp.79–80.
12. Psychiatric Hospital. *Plan of Recovery.* 1997: Author.
13. American Psychiatric Association. Pharm/alert notes, News for the Hospital Pharmacist. *Recognizing and Treating Depression* (p. 6), (1994) Washington: Author.
14. Psychiatric Hospital. *Mood Disorders and Depression,* year and author unknown.
15. Hospital Addiction Recovery Unit. *Plan of Recovery,* 1997: Author.
16. Psychiatric Hospital. *Spiritual Recovery,* author and year unknown.
17. Hospital Addiction Recovery Unit, New Life Recovery. *Medications in Recovery,* 1996: pp. 1–4. Author unknown.
18. Psychiatric Hospital. *Plan of Recovery,* 1997: Author.
19. Psychiatric Hospital. Video on *Stress Overload.* No other information available.
20. Robinson, R. (1997) pp. 2–4.

Chapter Thirteen

1. National Institute of Mental Health. *Depression: What Every Woman Should Know* (2005): p. 1. Author.
2. American Psychiatric Association. "Recognizing and Treating Depression" Alarm/alert notes, News for the Hospital Pharmacist. (1994): p. 6.
3. Spearing, M., of NIMH. *What are the Symptoms of Bipolar Disorder?* (2001): pp. 1–3, 6.
4. NIMH. *Depression: What Every Woman Should Know* (2005): pp. 3–5, Author.
5. Psychatric Hospital. *Mood Disorders and Depression,* 1996, Author.
6. Whybrow, Peter C., M.D. *A Mood Apart: Depression, Mania and Other Afflictions of the Self.* (1997) pp. 14–7. New York: Basic Books, HarperCollins.
7. Clark, D. In Whybrow, P. *A Mood Apart.* (1997) pp. 144–5.
8. Depression and Bipolar Support Alliance. *You've Just Been Diagnosed . . . What Now?* (2004): pp. 2–9. Author.
9. Papolos, Demitri, M.D. National Alliance for the Mentally Ill. *Mood Disorders, Depression and Manic Depression.* pp. 1–16. New York.
10. DBSA (2004): p. 9.
11. Spearing, M. of NIMH. (2001): p. 1.
12. NIMH (2002): p. 9.
13. Spearing, M. (2001): p. 2.
14. *Ibid.,* p. 2.
15. Whybrow, P., M.D. (1997): p. 136.
16. Spearing, M., NIMH, p. 2.
17. *Ibid.,* p. 5.
18. *Ibid., pp. 2–3.*
19. Whybrow, P. (1997): pp. 16–7.
20. NIMH, (2002): p. 13.
21. Peurifoy, R. (1995): p. 5.
22. Peale, Norman Vincent. *Thought Conditioners.* (1975) New York: Peale Center for Christian Living.
23. Bourne, E.J., Ph.D. (1996): pp. 7–8.
24. DBSA (2004): p. 16.
25. Bourne, E.J., Ph.D. (1996): p. 103.

Bibliography

Books

Bourne, Edmund J., Ph.D. *The Anxiety and Phobia Workbook, Second Edition, (1996). Oakland, CA: New Harbinger Publications, Inc.*

Clark, D. In Whybrow, P. Ph.D., *A Mood Apart: Depression, Mania and Other Afflictions of the Self.* (1997) New York: Basic Books, HarperCollins Publishing.

Duke, P. and Hochman, G. *A Brilliant Madness: Living with Manic Depressive Illness.* (1992) New York: Bantam Books.

Duke, P. and Turan, K. *Call Me Anna, The Autobiography of Patty Duke.* (1987) New York: Bantam Books.

Dyer, W. *Real Magic, Creating Miracles in Everyday Life.* (1987) New York: HarperCollins Publishing.

Peale, N.V. *Thought Conditioners.* (1975) New York: Peale Center for Christian Living.

Peurifoy, R.Z. *Anxiety, Phobias and Panic, A Step by Step Program for Regaining Control of Your Life.* New York: Warner Books.

Whybrow, Peter C., M.D. *A Mood Apart: Depression, Mania and other Afflictions of the Self.* New York: Basic Books, HarperCollins Publishing.

Pamphlets

Adult Services Treatment Program. *Patient Concern Resolution Guide,* 1996.

Hospital Addiction Recovery Unit, New Life Recovery. *Medications in Recovery,* 1996.

Psychiatric Hospital. *Mood Disorders and Depression,* 1996: Author.

Psychiatric Hospital. *Plan of Recovery,* 1997: Author.

Psychiatric Hospital. *Patient Rights,* 1997: Author.

Psychiatric Hospital. *Spiritual Recovery,* 1996: Author.

Robinson, R. Chronic Mental Illness, *Patient Education Manual,* 1997.

Articles

American Psychiatric Association. "Recognizing and Treating Depression," Pharm/alert notes, *News for the Hospital Pharmacist.* (1994): p. 6.

Depression and Bipolar Support Alliance. "You've Just Been Diagnosed . . . What Now?" (DBSA) (2004): pp. 2–9, 16.

National Institute of Mental Health. "A Story of Bipolar Disorder (manic depressive illness)" (2002): pp. 1–24.

National Institute of Mental Health, "Facts about Panic Disorder" (Sept. 1999): pp. 1–3.

Papolos, Demitri, M.D. National Alliance for the Mentally Ill. "Mood Disorders, Depression and Manic Depression" Year: pp. 1–16.

Spearing, M. of National Institute of Mental Health. "What are the Symptoms of Bipolar Disorder?" (2001): pp. 1–3, 99.

Newspaper

Union Recorder, "Uncovering the Central State Hospital Cemetery." (Sept. 1997): p. 14. Author.

Movie

Cayattes, Andre. *Le Miroir a Deux Faces.* 1958.

Cayattes, Andre and Oury, Gerad. *The Mirror Has Two Faces.* 1996.

Video

Psychiatric Hospital, *Stress Overload,* year and author unknown.